BENDING T

To the memory of those who fought, over the last
century, for a full and effective
system of public education,
now at risk

# Bending the Rules

*The Baker 'Reform' of Education*

## Brian Simon

LAWRENCE & WISHART
LONDON

Lawrence and Wishart Limited
39 Museum Street
London WC1A 1LQ

First published March 1988
Second edition May 1988
Third edition November 1988
© Brian Simon, 1988

Photoset in North Wales by
Derek Doyle and Associates, Mold, Clwyd.
Printed and bound in Great Britain by
Oxford University Press

# Contents

Introduction                                         7
Introduction to the Third Edition                    9

1  **Background and Objectives**

1  Thatcher's Objectives                            11
2  The Background – or, the Opportunity             19
3  The Comprehensive School                         29
4  Evidence from Scotland                           36
5  The Basis of Tory Policy                         41

2  **Destabilisng the Local Authorities:**
   **Open Enrolment and Opting Out**

1  An Interrelated Strategy                         47
2  'Consultation' and the Response                  56
3  Open Enrolment                                   59
4  Opting Out ('Grant Maintained Schools')          69
5  Financial Delegation and Charging for
   Extras                                           80
   (i)   Local Financial Management
   (ii)  Fees for 'Extras'

3  **Further Depredations**

1  Breaking up the ILEA                             89
2  Further and Higher Education                     95

4   **The Curriculum and Testing**

    1   The Proposals                                          107
    2   The Critique: Curriculum                               115
    3   The Critique of Testing                                122


5   **A Constitutional Issue?**                               137


6   **The Education Act and the Future**

    1   The Education Act, 1988                                153
    2   The Bill's Reception                                   158
    3   The Broad Alliance                                     160
    4   The Bill in Parliament                                 166
    5   Implementing the Act:                                  173
        (i)    Local Financial Management and
               Opting Out
        (ii)   City Technology Colleges
        (iii)  Curriculum and Testing
    6   Perspectives for the Future                            182

# Introduction

This book is written for parents as well as teachers, for school governors, administrators and advisers, for members of education committees of local authorities – indeed for all those who have the interests of the public system of education at heart. It sets out to explain, in comprehensible language, and in some detail, the real meaning of the Education Bill. It has been written in some haste – perhaps with some passion; but I have set out to be as objective as possible in dealing with the implications of the Bill, and hope that my personal feelings have not clouded my judgement. By profession an historian of education, I can say that at no previous period in the history of education have those who have its interests at heart been faced with so wide-ranging and ominous a challenge.

There are many to whom I owe debts of gratitude for their assistance. To Joan Simon, who put her own work aside to type the manuscript (a practice against *both* our principles, overridden in this case) and in so doing undoubtedly sharpened up its presentation. To Harry Rée and Clyde Chitty, both of whom have kept their eyes open and supplied me with essential material. To Harvey Goldstein and Roger Murphy, for discussions on key aspects of the proposals on assessment and testing. To Bob Borthwick, for discussion on constitutional issues.

Also to Alan Evans, and his staff at the National Union of Teachers, for essential documents, to Nora David and to Tessa Blackstone for encouragement, assistance and support. I wish to acknowledge also the continuous assistance of my colleagues on the Editorial Board of the independent educational journal *Forum* and in particular to that of my co-editor, Nanette Whitbread. But perhaps I should say at this stage that I must myself take full responsibility for what is written here.

A book of this kind must rely heavily on the press for accurate and up to date information on daily developments. Here I have to acknowledge, and thank, Peter Wilby and his team on the *Independent*, and Stuart Maclure and his colleagues at the *Times Educational Supplement*. The former have covered the inception of the Bill, and developments since, on a daily basis and in an exemplary manner, while in the weekly *TES* the editorial staff have maintained a consistent, informed and critical analysis of all aspects of the Bill's proposals, both in the initial 'consultation' papers and since.

Perhaps I should make it clear that the book is concerned with England and Wales only – it is here that the bulk of the Bill is directed; Scotland is only affected through the clauses dealing with universities, although the Scottish system is also currently under an attack which certainly deserves sharp critical analysis. Finally perhaps I should express my gratitude to Lawrence and Wishart; the book was their idea, not mine. It has involved intensive labour for several weeks. If it does something to clarify the issues at stake, and so to strengthen resistance to a measure that I believe will, if carried through Parliament in its original form, have a disastrous effect on our public system of education, that effort will have been very well worth while.

Brian Simon
9 December 1987

## Introduction to the Third Edition

This book was originally written in November 1987, when the Education 'Reform' Bill, now an Act, was originally published. The Bill passed through all stages in Parliament during the spring and summer of 1988, receiving Royal Assent on 29 July 1988. It is now part of the statutory laws of this country.

Although certain, relatively minor, changes were made in the Bill during its passage through Parliament, as far as the schools clauses in particular are concerned, the Act embodies, almost precisely, the government's intentions as first set out in the 'Consultation Papers' published shortly after the General Election, in July 1987. It is with these clauses that this book is largely concerned, although a short section deals also with Further and Higher Education. I believe that the critique of these clauses (especially those concerned with open enrolment, opting out, the curriculum and testing) retains its validity, together with the critique of the enhanced centralisation of control, as discussed in Chapter 5. These chapters are, therefore, reprinted unchanged from the original edition. The decision to abolish the Inner London Education Authority, of course, was taken after the publication of the original Bill, and is referred to in Chapter 6; the government's original proposals to allow Inner London boroughs to opt out of the ILEA are discussed in Chapter 3.

The original Chapter 6, 'The Fightback and the Alternative' has, however, been fully revised for this edition. The actual passage of the Bill has rendered some of the original chapter out of date, while new developments since its passage require analysis. This sixth chapter is, therefore, largely revised and rewritten, and contains new material.

The clause numbering in the first five chapters refers to clause numbers in the original Bill. Chapter 6 contains at the start a brief analysis of the main sections of the Act, as finally passed, giving the section numbers as presented there.

The passage of the Education 'Reform' Act creates a new situation. It was a main argument of the original edition of this book that passage of the Bill, if virtually unchanged during the Parliamentary process, would put at risk the main gains achieved in the field of education over the last decades. But implementation of so unpopular a measure, in the full sense clearly desired by the present government, may not prove altogether easy. Indeed the defence of systems of primary and secondary comprehensive education under local (democratic) control may prove a rallying point leading to their strengthening and even extension. The force, power and conviction of those believing in the equal provision of a public good – in this case, education – may prove great enough to resist its erosion, through imposition of the ideology of the market place – the competitive theory that powers and underlies this Act. As suggested in the last chapter, outcomes may be unexpected. How things in fact work out will depend on the struggles of the future.

Brian Simon
18 September 1988

# 1 Background and Objectives

## 1 Thatcher's Objectives

'The Great Education Reform Bill', as Kenneth Baker likes to describe it, was first officially announced in Parliament in the Queen's speech at the end of June, three weeks after the Tories' massive (electoral) victory at the General Election on 11 June 1987. Its main features had been embodied in the Conservative manifesto, and announced by Margaret Thatcher, Kenneth Baker and others during the campaign (though not without som . confusion on the issue of charging fees in maintained schools). 'Tories: We'll End Schools Tyranny', headlined the *Daily Mail* on 13 May. The manifesto 'reveals a radical determination effectively to extend the privatisation programme into the state education monolith', wrote Gordon Greig, political editor. 'We are going much further with education than we had ever thought of going before,' Thatcher told her favourite editor, Sir David English, in an exclusive interview a few hours after she announced the election date. 'You mean there is going to be a revolution in the running of the schools if you are re-elected?' 'That's right,' answered Thatcher. 'Money would flow to good schools and to good headmasters (*sic*).' Her overall aim, she concluded, was the 'elimination of socialism' and a

11

new political alignment – a two-party system with a Labour Party committed to 'the high ideals of freedom and democracy', but 'totally non-socialist'. Her education programme, she made clear, had a central part in the realisation of this perspective.

The unexpectedly large electoral victory in June, when the Tories polled 42 per cent of the vote but gained 60 per cent of seats in the Commons, raised new perspectives in Thatcher's planning for the future – the prospect of a fourth term to enable completion of her political 'revolution'. The election results had given a new confidence – already the main issue was to prepare the ground for the next election. 'Just as we gained political support in the last election from people who had acquired their own homes and shares,' she now claimed, 'so we shall secure still further our political base in 1991-92 – by giving people a real say in education and housing.' The proposed Education Bill is 'the key to the future: the biggest and most important legislation of the forthcoming parliamentary session' (*Independent*, 17 July 1987).

The most profound concern has been expressed by all organisations directly concerned with education at the unseemly haste with which the government has pursued its educational objectives. A series of 'consultation' papers, covering the main proposed measures, was issued at the end of July (though promised earlier), responses to be returned to the Department of Education and Science (DES) within two months, by the end of September. Parents (in whose name the legislation was being prepared) with children at home on holiday could hardly be reached for consultation; their organisations unanimously protested – what was the need for all this hurry? The churches (Anglican, Catholic, Methodist), local authorities (responsible for local systems), teachers' organisations, the TUC and labour movement organisations, all added their voice to these protests. August and early September were in no sense a practical moment for widespread consultation on issues of absolutely crucial importance for the future of the system. But all to no avail. 'We are a very strong government,' Thatcher told Peter Jenkins of the *Independent* in an interview on education in September. They knew what they wanted and were clearly intending to drive their plans through parliament, relying on populist support and the 100-plus majority in the Commons.

'Why all this hurry?' people asked. The reason has already been made clear. The Education Bill was seen as an overtly political measure. Its primary objective was to act as a springboard for the return of a Tory government at the next election probably four years later – and the longed-for fourth term for Margaret Thatcher. To get the measures through Parliament and actually operating in practice could in fact be done in three or in some cases four years – not less. Hence the urgency, the need to get the first steps under way with the utmost rapidity. No concessions were to be made, whatever the protests.

This, then, is primarily a political measure; it is recognised and even presented as such by the Prime Minister, and is now increasingly seen in this light by those directly concerned with education. Its aim is to achieve a decisive political advantage over other parties. This is not to say that, in the world of education, there are not important issues which need action – and quickly. These will be referred to later. It is only to say that the solution of educational problems is not the primary aim of this legislation. The primary aim is political.

There is here a sharp contrast with two of the three main Education Acts passed this century, those of 1944 (the Butler Act) and 1918 (the Fisher Act). Both of these Acts were consensus measures, carried with the support of *all* parties (in the case of the 1944 Act, including Conservative, Liberal, Labour and Communist), and of the churches, which had (and have) a considerable stake in education. In both cases the Acts were passed after at least two years of consultations. In 1942 and 1943, for instance, all organisations that so wished had time and opportunity to sort out their proposals in detail, to publish and circulate them, and to enter into discussions with the Minister who at least did them the honour of taking them seriously. Butler's discussions with the churches, for instance, were lengthy and detailed, resulting in a compromise that has stood the test of time.[1] But there were also lengthy consultations with the local authorities and the teachers, without whose support no new scheme could function with maximum effectiveness. And this was during a war, when the country was fighting for its very existence, against a real and ruthless enemy. Whatever problems arose within the education system with the passage of time, both these Acts were celebrated by all political parties, and by all those concerned professionally with education, as representing major advances.

The third main Education Act, the earliest in the century, that of 1902, was an exception. This Act (the Balfour Act) was driven through by a government comprising a large Tory majority in the teeth of determined opposition from both the Liberals and the nascent Labour Party. This Act put paid to democratic advances in the cities (particularly – interestingly – in the North) and alienated Nonconformists (mainly Liberal supporters) by putting church schools on the rates. As in the present case, this was an overtly *political* measure, fought out through education. Tremendous opposition was aroused throughout the country during its passage through Parliament. It may now be worth recalling (perhaps as a warning) that the passage of this Act was a major factor in the total defeat of the Tory party at the 1906 General Election – won by the Liberals who were returned with an overwhelming majority. The lesson of history, then, is that partisan politics in education may not pay.

What are the immediate, educational objectives of the proposed legislation? Once again these have been made abundantly clear by Margaret Thatcher. They are twofold. First, to break the power of the local authorities which traditionally have been directly responsible for running their own 'systems' of education (by far their largest responsibility, incidentally), and second to erect (or reinforce) an hierarchical system of schooling both subject to market forces and more directly under central state control. The contradiction apparent between these two latter objectives is well encapsulated in Thatcher's definition of the new proposed subsystem as comprising 'independent state schools'.

To take the latter objective first – the aim, as Thatcher defined it in July to the *Independent*, is to create a new 'system' of schools between the independent ('public' and private) schools for the wealthy, and the remnant of popular schools for the masses left with the local authorities. This new 'system' of schools, independent of local authorities, state financed, but partially subject to market forces, is designed to serve the needs of the yuppie and other sections of the middle strata. The objective of equal provision of a public resource (education) under local democratic control is totally rejected. 'You are going to have *three* systems,' Thatcher told the *Independent*. 'First there will be those who wish to stay with the local authority', then 'you are going to have direct grant schools' (funded directly by the state, B.S.), 'and then you are going to have a private sector with assisted places'. 'That', she said, 'is variety.' It would give 'a wider choice of public provision' for 'people who are not satisfied'.

The objective of downgrading and bypassing local authorities to establish a whole mini-'system' of quasi-independent schools has also been clearly spelt out by Kenneth Baker as Minister. Here again the appeal is to 'variety'. 'I want a much greater degree of variety and independence in the running of schools,' Baker told Stuart Maclure, editor of the *Times Educational Supplement* (3 April 1987). 'I want to see a greater amount of variety and choice.' About 7 per cent or so go to independent schools, he said later, 93 per cent to the state maintained sector. 'I'm responsible for that. What I think is striking in the British educational system is that there is nothing in between.' The proposed city technology colleges 'are a half-way house. I would like to see many more half-way houses, a greater choice, a greater variety. I think many parents would as well.' (*TES*, 3 April 1987)

By appealing to 'variety' and 'choice' Baker and Thatcher are utilising a long established Tory ploy. In the past this argument was used to legitimise the tripartite system, as well as to give support to voluntary (church) schools when these were under attack. Today it is used to legitimise a variety of types or levels of schools, subsidised from public funds in various, often hidden ways, e.g. through the assisted places scheme, sometimes charging fees, and designed for intermediate social strata – professional, business and technocratic. While the Tories want a *variety* of schools, however, they are also arguing for a strict *uniformity* in the curriculum where, they now claim, there is too much 'variety'.

Developing a new structure of schooling leads directly to the major objective – the more or less total erosion of the powers and responsibilities of local authorities. This also has been clearly stated, time and again, by Margaret Thatcher and her acolytes – and in this area no holds are barred in an outright populist appeal. The attack on local government, including severe rate-capping, has gone on a long time – ever since a ruthless centralising thrust became apparent under the previous Secretary of State, Keith Joseph, and, as will be argued in Chapter 5, even earlier. A new opportunity was, however, provided recently by the supposedly exaggerated actions of a small minority of left-wing dominated Labour Councils – Brent, Haringey and perhaps Camden – the so-called 'loony left', of which much was made in the mass media. Here the poll tax is presented as one solution; encouraging schools to 'opt out' from the local authority is another. 'The power of the local authorities would be reduced,' Thatcher told David English in May (*Daily Mail*, 13 May 1987); over the last few years 'we have seen a kind of extreme left-wing local authority' of a kind not seen before. The aim would be 'to get some of these schools out of the local authorities and have direct grants from the Department of Education', and, she added, where parents were in open revolt against subjects like gay studies 'she would act'. 'I don't like what is going on,' the Prime Minister continued, 'and that is exactly why we would be taking the powers from the local authorities in these cases.'

But, as things have turned out, it is not only 'in these cases' that action is proposed, but for local authorities as a whole – Tory, 'hung' (as many are today), Liberal and Labour; the target is very clearly the entire historically developed and traditional system of local government as a whole. It is well known that Margaret Thatcher hopes or believes that, through legislation, the great majority of schools will 'opt out', leaving the authorities with the rump. Any argument is good enough to denigrate local authorities as a whole. This campaign of abuse reached its apogee at the Conservative Party conference early in October 1987. In her 'Presidential' address Thatcher claimed that children 'particularly in inner cities' had a true education 'all too often snatched from them by hard-left education authorities and extremist teachers'. Children were being taught 'anti-racist mathematics, political slogans, that they had an inalienable right to be gay and that our society offered them no future'. Stressing proposals for opting out she went on to say, with evident hostility, that 'There's no reason at all why local authorities should have a monopoly of free education. What principle suggests this is right? What recent experience or practice suggests it is even sensible?' (*Guardian*, 10 October 1987)

These arguments spurred the normally sober and moderate editorial staff of the *Times Educational Supplement* to an indignant response. Mrs Thatcher's arguments were 'intellectually disreputable'. Her charges lay far from the truth. 'How many classes are there in session this Friday morning?' the editorial asked. 'A quarter of a million or thereabouts?' And in 'just how many does Mrs T seriously believe children are being taught "anti-racist maths, political slogans and the virtues of homosexuality?".' If her policy were really based on nothing more than 'malicious, sensational, tittle-tattle' we really would be in a mess. Sooner or later Mr Baker had to try and win the respect of educators for his programme. 'This is going to be difficult enough without Mrs Thatcher's insults.' (*TES*, 16 October 1987)

But what Thatcher was up to was mounting a populist attack (with the aid of the tabloid press) on local government as a whole, the destabilisation of which is a central concern of current legislation. 'The return of a Conservative government today', forecast Peter Wilby of the *Independent* on election day, 'will mean the break-up of the state education system that has existed since 1944.' Whether this prophecy proves true or not depends on the struggles over the Baker 'Reform' Bill; but that this is the clear intention cannot be in doubt.

## 2 The Background – or, the Opportunity

We have so far tackled two questions – first, why this extreme urgency to get the Education 'Reform' Bill through Parliament? Second, what are the major Thatcherite objectives? It is now important to set these current moves in context. What is the background to these startling developments? How is it that education has become a major political issue? The 'ordinary people of England' want the schools reformed, Kenneth Baker is reported as saying recently in a talk to 'colleagues at Westminster and in Whitehall who are opposed to the scheme', and he was going to get that reform through 'without any fudging or dilution'. This front page *Daily Mail* story carried an inch high headline: 'Nothing Will Stop Us Now' (15 September 1987). What is the basis for this apparent confidence in popular support?

It is, of course, common knowledge that there has been a great deal of criticism of the schools over the last ten to fifteen years – especially from certain big industrialists and politicians. The start of this criticism coincided with the oil crisis in the mid-1970s, and reached its apogee in the period of massive de-industrialisation accompanied by mass unemployment, which particularly hit young people, in the early 1980s. The country had invested generously in education in the 1960s, motivated by increasing demand reflecting enhanced aspirations of 'ordinary people', and by the then popular and widely accepted 'human capital theory' by which the country's leading economists held that investment in education increased the stock of 'human capital' which is the key to enhanced productivity and economic growth. But soon after, the economic crises of the 1970s put paid to these apparently over-enthusiastic aspirations. It appeared that education had 'failed' – and this was the message emblazoned in the headlines of the tabloid press and repeated, perhaps more discreetly, in the quality papers and on television. The chase was on.

Of course not even the most optimistic of the economists ever argued that increased investment in education would or could lead to an *immediate* increase in output or gross national product. Education is a process, the outcome of which in terms of increased abilities and skills, the growth of science and knowledge generally, its application in advanced technology, must inevitably take time – be spread over decades rather than years. But the immediacy – indeed suddenness – of the crisis that shook this country, together with others, forced a search for a scapegoat. Industrialists, whose confidence was shaken, turned on the schools. These, it was claimed, were failing to produce young people with the skills required by industry. It was not industry or industrialists that were at fault; still less the economic and financial system as a whole. It was the schools – and, it followed, the teachers and the local authorities responsible for local systems. So a widespread attack, and critique, was mounted.

This approach was both enhanced and legitimised by leading politicians. The speech by the then Prime Minister, James Callaghan, at Ruskin College, Oxford in October 1976 has gone down in history as marking the start of a veritable campaign to make schools more responsive to industry, and above all to make them more 'accountable' to parents, the public and the government. The intention was to shake the system into line.

This is not the place to go into the history of these last ten years – the experience of growing conflict and demoralisation, of unexpected initiatives, of exhortation and clamour. Some of the main issues, however, do require special attention.

The brunt of the attack was directed at secondary education – specifically at the new system of comprehensive schools now educating the bulk of all pupils of secondary school age. Primary education – until recently seen as the jewel in the crown of British education, and much admired in the USA and elsewhere – was also subjected to criticism (sometimes vitriolic abuse), in particular for the use of 'modern methods' as celebrated in the Plowden Report of 1967. But it was the comprehensive secondary schools that were held to be most culpable. Television programmes (including those of the BBC) presented 'typical' comprehensives as chaotic – their teachers as both unpleasant and incompetent. Parental criticisms, where these surfaced, were given mass treatment in the tabloid press. Criticism was directed at these schools both from the right, which had never accepted them (for instance, in the whole series of so-called 'Black Papers' in the 1970s), and from the left (for instance in *Unpopular Education*, a 1981 publication of the Centre for Contemporary Cultural Studies at Birmingham University). Sociologists added to the hue and cry – these schools were not achieving the social and economic equality their progenitors claimed.[2] Social scientists now claimed that education in any case could make 'no difference' to the inequalities embedded in contemporary society (the Jencks and Coleman Reports);[3] education necessarily had the function of reinforcing existing inequalities, and ensuring the perpetuation of hierarchical structures, argued neo-Marxists like Althusser, sociologists like Bourdieu and their English counterparts. All this led to further demoralisation in the schools. What, then, had the comprehensive reform been about? What was the point of it all?

The swing to comprehensive education was a deeply rooted, grass-roots movement which originated among local authorities and took off with accelerating force from about 1963. It represented the determination of the mass of 'ordinary people' to get rid of the 11-plus examination and the divided structure of secondary education, accompanied by rigid streaming of pupils in primary schools from the age of seven (or even earlier) in a system by which children's life chances were determined by their stream placement on entry to the junior school. The 11-plus involved the rejection of over 70 per cent of the nation's children who were relegated to secondary modern schools, which had no connections with higher education or the professions, at the age of eleven. The comprehensive school, to which all but a few children proceeded automatically without selection, was the evident solution. Eased by the 'liberal' thinking of Edward Boyle as the Tory minister up to 1964, and by both Boyle and Edward Heath, the leader of the Tory opposition in the late 1960s, and in spite of sharp institutional resistance by grammar schools and right-wing Tories, the comprehensive solution became almost a consensus policy in the 1960s and later. When Margaret Thatcher became Secretary of State for Education for the years from 1970, she was quite unable to stop or reverse the movement, even though she did succeed in throwing various spanners into the works (as described in *Indictment of Margaret Thatcher*, PSW (Educational) Publications, 1973). More schools went comprehensive during her period as minister (1970-74) than either before or after. The comprehensive school was a 'roller coaster' during her period, she is reported as saying recently. Plans made under the previous Labour government, by both Tory and Labour councils, were now being realised – it was not then practical politics even to consider stopping it.

But during the mid-to-late 1970s, comprehensive education ran into difficulties. It was now that the criticism referred to developed, that attacks were launched of unexampled ferocity, particularly on comprehensive schools in inner cities. And all was not well within the schools. In 1972 the school leaving age was raised to sixteen, allowing for a full five-year course for *all* students within comprehensive schools. But the structural reform was not accompanied by new thinking about the nature of education appropriate for all within the single school. Above all, the traditional grammar school,

university-orientated General Certificate of
Education (GCE) exam at the ages of sixteen and
eighteen ensured the perpetuation of a highly
academic content of studies within comprehensive
schools, even if the Certificate of Secondary
Education (CSE), a new exam for those considered
incapable of GCE brought in in 1963, provided an
alternative. In fact students within comprehensive
schools were split three ways. A minority pursued
the dominant academic path through GCE, a larger
'middle' group entered for CSE, while for the rest
(the bottom 40 per cent according to Keith Joseph)
there was nothing. The result, both of this situation
and, of course, of wider and more significant forms of
rejection ou⁺side the schools, was the massive
alienation from the schools' objectives of a substantial proportion of the students who found no clear
purpose for their studies. Such disaffection
enhanced problems of discipline – of the provision of
conditions conducive to orderly learning – led to
truancy on an increasing scale among the older age
groups and so contributed to the image of the
'failing' school.

All this was evident by 1979 when the Conservatives returned to power, with the one-time
Secretary of State for Education, Margaret
Thatcher, as Prime Minister. For a short period
things eased, although the new government's first
action was to get two Education Bills through
Parliament, both damaging to comprehensive
schools and to the maintained system in general.
The first abrogated a Labour measure requiring the
few local authorities which had not produced plans
to go comprehensive to produce them. The second,
more wide-ranging, had two objectives; first, to
enhance the private sector by introducing the

'Assisted Places Scheme', whereby public money is funded directly to students at independent schools,[4] and second, to increase the scope for parental choice within the maintained system (thereby enhancing differentiation within local systems of comprehensive education). This latter measure was supported by a populist appeal to the benefits arising from such 'choice' in enhancing the quality of education – good schools drive out bad, in contradistinction to Gresham's law.

But it was with the appointment in 1981 of Sir Keith Joseph, Thatcherite monetarist guru, that the attack on the schools – and on local authorities and especially on teachers as a profession – really got under way. There is no doubt whatsoever that, during his period of office which lasted four years, Keith Joseph (now ennobled) inflicted enormous damage on the educational service of the country. In particular he succeeded, through single-minded pursuit of doctrinaire monetary policies, in alienating not only the great bulk of the teaching profession, but also the local authorities and others concerned in the service. During his period of office the schools and colleges were systematically allowed to deteriorate in terms of buildings, maintenance and equipment, to levels not previously known. At the same time a consistent and ruthless thrust towards centralised control – over the curriculum, initial and in-service teacher training and in many other ways – eroded not only traditional partnership patterns, but, as an inevitable concomitant, wrenched the heart out of both local authority- and teacher-led initiatives. The pressure to bring all such developments within the control of central authority, initiated by Joseph and now carried much further by Baker, has been relentless.

What was the very real legacy of Sir Keith Joseph's long tenure at the Department of Education and Science?

First, an enormous mass of under-resourced and deteriorating ('crummy' in Joseph's phrase) school and college buildings throughout the country – a deterioration it will take years to overcome. It is well known that Joseph, during his term of office, was the only spending minister who *never* went into the so-called 'Star Chamber' – the Cabinet committee which finally arbitrates on government expenditure – to argue for more money for education. This is because, as a confirmed monetarist, he simply could not bring himself to make such a plea – or case. Spending on school buildings in fact fell by a massive 35 per cent in the years 1981-86, so that the Parliamentary Committee on Education, Science and the Arts estimated in 1986 that a £700,000,000 backlog on maintenance had built up. Joseph argued that high quality education can go on in 'crummy' buildings. (Did he have Harrow, unsurprisingly his own school, in mind?) The devastation so created is such that these are becoming the only buildings.

Second, an alienated teaching profession. In a speech in January, 1985 (to the North of England education conference) Joseph's managerial view of teachers was stressed at the start. 'Today I shall speak mostly about teachers, the main agents for the delivery of the curriculum.' As a Chief Education Officer (Jackson Hall) argued, the Secretary of State should seek to have 500,000 allies, not 500,000 'agents' (*Forum*, Vol. 28, No.1). This contempt for teachers and their role came out very clearly in Joseph's statements about the need for 'appraisal' and his continued linking of appraisal with differential rates of pay. Joseph was apparently incapable of saying a good word for teachers – of implying any degree of respect for them and their work. This attitude, together with his monetarism, lay behind the hard line he took on the salary issue, leading to the year-long teachers' action, the net effect of which was to inflict enormous damage on the schools, and bring about the more or less total alienation of the profession – conditions only now gradually beginning to be overcome.

Third, enhanced central control. A whole series of actions by Keith Joseph was deliberately designed to shift the focus of power decisively to the centre, at the expense of both local authorities and teachers. Examples include the summary abolition of the Schools Council (responsible for curriculum and examinations) where both teachers and local authorities were well represented, and its substitution by two nominated quangos to carry out government policy on curriculum and examinations, an action manifesting contempt for the involvement of others in the determination of these crucial educational questions. The abolition of the Central Advisory Councils for England and Wales by the 1986 Act is another case in point – and this without any suggestion for the establishment of any organisation which could draw both on expert and public opinion and act in an advisory capacity to the politicians and civil servants. The right of local authorities to determine their own in-service policies was removed by utilising new systems of central funding to impose centrally determined priorities. Under Joseph, and with his overt connivance, the Manpower Services Commission was brought in to finance and mastermind centrally imposed curriculum development (the Technical and Vocational Educational Initiative). Precise, centrally determined criteria were to be

established governing examining (and so teaching
and the curriculum) in the new, single exam, the
General Certificate of Secondary Education. Even
this list could be greatly extended. The damage done
to the concept and practice of 'partnership' started
under Joseph, and now threatening to be taken
much further under Baker, will certainly rever-
berate far into the future. We will revert to this
important constitutional issue in Chapter 5.

Keith Joseph constantly reiterated, throughout
his period of office, that his main concern was with
'standards', with the *quality* of education. But
towards the end of his period matters had reached
such a point that the Secretary of State nearly
brought the entire edifice crumbling down around
him. His long swan-song (from 2 Febuary 1986,
when he first announced his retirement, to the end
of May) with the teachers' action still grumbling on,
the schools in increasing disarray, brought demands
right across the spectrum – from the *Daily
Telegraph* to the *Guardian* – that he should go and
go quickly. Then, very suddenly, in March that year,
education became a national issue. Now for a couple
of months right-wing Tory politicians and press had
a field day in the promulgation of every kind of
hare-brained scheme to solve the problem of the
so-called 'failure' of the existing system – in
particular several variants of voucher schemes (by
which parents are given the cost of their child's
education and shop around for a congenial school)
rejected as impracticable by Joseph. Carefully
organised leaks revealed that Thatcher and Joseph
were to bring in 'Crown schools', direct grant inner
city primary schools, selective technical schools and
the like – a veritable witches' brew. The municipal
elections in early May 1986 injected a note of

realism, however. The shocking state of the schools throughout the country was, all commentators agreed, one of the main reasons for the massive defeats inflicted on the Conservative Party throughout the country.[5] This hit the Tories where it hurt most, at the polls. Something had to be done, and done quickly. From a vote-loser the Tories were determined to transform education into a vote-winner. But how was this to be done?

We will leave this question here for the moment and turn our attention to a related matter – the schools themselves and particularly the comprehensive secondary schools, now catering for over 90 per cent of students within the maintained system in England, and 95 per cent in Wales.

## 3  The Comprehensive School

It may seem odd that, in spite of all that has been said concerning their very real problems and difficulties, and in spite of constant media criticism and attacks, reinforced by a continuing stream of complaints by industrialists and leading politicians, comprehensive secondary (and primary) schools have generally been working well – or as well as could be expected given the severe cutbacks experienced. Generally comprehensive schools have many successes to their credit. Where they have failed is in getting these across nationally. Teachers and others have come to realise that the media (including the 'quality' papers) are interested in disasters, not in the quiet success of even-handed action. But this does not go for local communities who know their schools, often intimately. Local support for comprehensives, even in the most unlikely areas, has been overwhelming, as we shall see.

Examination results are admittedly a narrow criterion, and open to considerable criticism from many points of view. But these are often appealed to by those who claim that comprehensive education leads to a decline in 'standards'. What is the position here?

To compare the position in 1984-85 to that fourteen years earlier (1970-71), when less than half the secondary students were in comprehensive schools in the United Kingdom, we find that:

1. The percentage of the age cohort gaining five or more GCE O Levels at grades A to C (or their equivalent) – often used as the basic measure as regards trends in standards – has increased by over 45 per cent (from 7.1 to 10.3 per cent). This is a very substantial advance which coincides with a rapid swing to comprehensive education.

2. The percentage gaining from one to four O Levels at grades A to C (or their equivalent) has increased by 60 per cent (from 16.8 to 26.8 per cent).

3. The percentage gaining one or more O Levels at grades D or E, or CSE grades 2 to 5, has increased by over 200 per cent (from 9.8 to 32.5 per cent).

4. Conversely, the percentage gaining no passes at whatever level in GCE or CSE has dramatically declined – from 44 per cent (or almost half) in 1970-71 to 11.7 per cent fourteen years later.[6]

The fact that no qualifications whatever were offered (during the period covered) to over a tenth of the students, and the inappropriateness of some of the actual qualifications mentioned above is another issue altogether. The point to be stressed is the very positive achievements of the schools over what was a very difficult and in many ways demoralising period. The credit for this must go to the schools, to the students themselves and above all to the teachers whose achievement it is. This success is also reflected in GCE Advanced Level results, which have improved by nearly 10 per cent over the period examined, so that in 1984-85, 18.1 per cent of school leavers gained one or more A Levels (or, in Scotland, SCE H grades).

More will be said on exam results shortly, in the light of some striking evidence from Scotland only very recently available. But let us look now at the issue of local support for comprehensive education. Here also the evidence is striking.

In the autumn of 1983 a public opinion poll, reported in the press, seemed to indicate that a majority of those questioned supported the selective grammar/secondary modern school set-up in preference to comprehensives. This was given very wide publicity, as was to be expected of any news critical of comprehensive education. The outcome was predictable. Some 60 Tory MPs, seeing perhaps electoral advantage, signed a Parliamentary motion favouring return to selective education. In addition one of the Ministers at the Department of Education and Science (Robert Dunn) made a series of weekend speeches advocating a return to grammar schools.

Solihull was among a number of Tory-controlled local authorities which leapt on to the bandwagon, proposing the transformation of two successful comprehensives into grammar schools. The fact that all the other schools would, in effect, be downgraded as secondary moderns was nowhere mentioned. But what immediately became clear was that those in control had totally failed to evaluate the feeling among the local population in support of their schools. There was a massive outcry – large meetings took place at which enormous majorities voted clearly against the council's proposals; in

particular very effective joint activity by parents
(who set up a defence association) and teachers'
associations, especially the National Union of
Teachers, was a feature of the campaign.

In the face of this opposition the original scheme
was withdrawn, but, in an attempt to save face and
retrieve something from the wreckage, a second
scheme was presented, now proposing that one
school only should be transformed. But this again
met with a further massive outcry, together with a
very effective campaign launched by the local NUT
association in co-operation with parents and the
local communities. So this scheme also had to be
abandoned.

Solihull had opted, and in a very clear manner, to
retain its comprehensives. From that moment, no
more has been heard of the original project. Here
was a clear and precise public test as to the degree of
support there is for local comprehensive systems -
the first on this scale (and, since then, no other
authority has attempted to turn the clock back like
this). Whatever people may say to public opinion
pollsters, whose questions relate to abstract issues
and are carefully worded, when the matter comes
down to earth in an attempt to destroy local systems
(no less), comprehensive education, it seems, can
call on a really massive degree of support. This is the
lesson from the Solihull adventure.

But developments went further than this. At this
time (1984) concurrent attempts in Berkshire and
Wiltshire to extend still existing selective procedures met with an equally unyielding opposition
from local people, again involving mass meetings
and consistent pressure on Tory councillors. In both
cases local populations opted to retain non-selective
procedures and, in effect, to defend existing

comprehensive schools and systems. At Redbridge also an overt attempt to turn back the clock and reintroduce (or extend) selective schooling again met with a public outcry, and a clear rejection by the majority living in this area.

Evidently, then, those who set out to disrupt and, in effect, directly to sabotage existing comprehensive systems, have been forced to retire with bloody noses. And this was as recently as the autumn of 1984. At this point comprehensive education defeated a determined and powerful challenge to its popularity and emerged with flying colours. This was clearly the moment when the Tory government realised that the policy of direct disruption was politically unacceptable. From this point also dates the alternative dual policy of reinforcing differentiation *within* the single (comprehensive) school,[7] and *circumventing* local systems by the establishment of new (selective) schools alongside them, e.g. city technology colleges, and *destabilising* local systems by encouraging the most successful local schools to 'opt out' of local authority control. But this is to trespass on the subject of the next chapter.

There is a good deal of further evidence of local support for comprehensives, although one has to read the press reports carefully to find this out — even in the 'quality' press the journalists (or sub-editors) present this evidence under strongly negative headlines. Thus in the *Independent* (sadly), under the very typical heading 'Parents' Faith in School Declines', we learn that 'seven out of ten parents' (that makes 70 per cent in my calculation) 'are either satisfied or very satisfied with their children's schools', while eight out of ten parents (i.e. 80 per cent!) 'thought schools *academically good, well-organised* and *well-disciplined*' (my emphasis,

B.S.). This enquiry focussed on parents of thirteen-
and fourteen-year-olds attending secondary schools
in the Inner London Education Authority Area (14
January 1987).[8]

Finally let us examine carefully the result of a
Gallup Opinion Poll specially commissioned by the
*Daily Telegraph* early in October 1987 – timed to
coincide with the Conservative Party conference and
clearly designed to provide support for current
government policies (7 October 1987). In the
outcome, only the headlines (once again) provided
that support; the bulk of the actual data supported
the opposite view. Indeed the way this poll was
reported provides an object lesson in the unscrupu-
lous journalistic tactics utilised by the press as a
whole throughout this period.

Directly under the heading 'Poll Backs Plans for
Schools' we are informed that 'one parent in five is
dissatisfied with standards at school and a similar
number would like to opt out of local authority
control'. That makes 20 per cent. Presumably then,
we can infer that as high a proportion as *80 per cent*
are in fact *satisfied* with 'standards at school' and
have no desire to opt out of local authority control
(actually we are told on another page that 60 per
cent would not want their school to 'opt out'). Was
not this news worth directly reporting – particularly
at that precise moment in time? Later we are told
'Overall, a quarter of parents believe standards have
dropped over the last few years, with bad teaching,
poor discipline and the effect of financial cuts most
commonly blamed.' No one would deny that all three
of these factors are operative, but the 'good news' is
that, even in the teeth of financial cuts etc. the poll
in fact reveals that *three-quarters* of those questioned did *not* think 'standards have dropped', and

this might have provided a more accurate headline. Clearly the *Daily Telegraph* had a hot line to Kenneth Baker at the Tory conference. Under a sub-head 'Message "Getting Across"' Mr Baker is reported as saying that 'the poll proved the government was getting the message across about its new proposals'. Did it?[9]

But there is further information from this poll related to current policies which might (should?) interest Mr Baker and Mrs Thatcher. Under the headline 'Parents Support Exam Shake-up in State Schools' we find, if hidden away, that 46 per cent said that *teachers* should 'wield the greatest influence over running schools'; a further 25 per cent favoured *local authorities* having 'the greatest influence' (together that makes 71 per cent) and *'only 5 per cent said that the government should play the largest part'* (my emphasis, B.S.). (That covers 76 per cent of the responses.) The report continued: 'Only one in five (19 per cent) called for parents to wield the greatest influence.' We are later told that 'Only a tiny proportion (7 per cent) say that they have actually been refused a place at the school of their choice.'

This data, looked at objectively, amounts to a popular rejection of the whole basis of current government policies. The only majority support for such policies it reveals is for the concept of a 'core curriculum' (almost two-thirds of the sample of parents), and for the introduction of 'national written tests' in English, maths and science at the ages of seven, eleven and fourteen (71 per cent). These issues will be discussed in Chapter 4. But as far as structural change is concerned and its supposed basis ('failure' of the schools, widespread parental dissatisfaction, frustration and dismay), this, the most recent full opinion poll as I write, presents a picture *the precise opposite* of the myths press and politicians have assiduously and, as I suggested earlier, *unscrupulously propagated consistently and relentlessly now for a period of ten or more years*. The conclusion must be that, in spite of their problems which have been awesome, and in spite of certain evident weaknesses, the schools, as they actually exist, are deeply rooted in their neighbourhoods and enjoy a very high degree of support. It may be appropriate here to quote the view of Barry Taylor, a highly respected and energetic Chief Education Officer, for Somerset, who sadly died very recently at the age of 51, in a talk to the Secondary Heads Association in the spring of 1984. The achievements of secondary schools, he is reported as saying,

> are remarkable, despite the upheaval caused by the switch to comprehensive education and a background of unemployment, rapid technological and social change, shortage of resources and social instability. Those of us with responsibility for secondary education need not feel defensive. *Secondary schools are currently meeting the daunting challenges which our society represents in a way which is a major success story, not a catalogue of failure. (Guardian*, 9 April 1984, my emphasis, B.S.)

## 4 Evidence from Scotland

Finally, we may look at the latest evidence available as to the 'success' or otherwise of comprehensive education. This is a typically systematic study of comprehensive education in Scotland, involving three 'cohorts' of students (leaving school in 1976, 1980 and 1984) each representative of the majority of Scottish schools and each comprising a large sample, totalling 40,000 in all. The study was carried through by Andrew McPherson at the Centre for Educational Sociology at the University of Edinburgh, where earlier comparable studies have been made. *No* similar comprehensive, research-based studies have been mounted in England and Wales, but the authors insist that it is reasonable to infer that the trends they have found in Scotland will be reflected, if to a lesser extent, in England and Wales. Research material is not everyone's cup of tea, but this is of real importance and the reader is asked to stay with the text. Every effort will be made to present the results simply and as clearly as possible.[10]

Comprehensive reorganisation took place more rapidly in Scotland than in England, and comprehends a greater proportion of students. But, the authors argue, 'It was not until the mid-1970s that the majority of pupils [in Scotland] could start their secondary schooling in a settled comprehensive system.' Earlier investigations had shown that the traditional Scottish 'omnibus' (basically non-selective) school softened class differences in educational attainment compared to the more rigid differences persisting in areas served by selective schooling. What the authors were concerned to investigate was whether any new trends could be discovered among students whose entire school life was spent in comprehensive schools in the more settled atmosphere from the mid-1970s.

Their main conclusions can be briefly summarised. Two distinct trends were found to have been operating since the mid-1970s. First, a general rise in average attainment (or 'standards') across all social classes, from the professional to the unskilled, and second, as the authors put it, 'a fall in the effect

*Figure 1: Average Attainment by Social Class in Scotland, 1976, 1980, 1984*

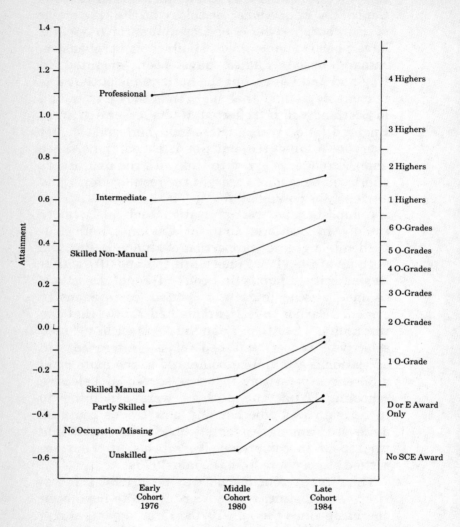

*Source:* Andrew McPherson and J. Douglas Willans, 'Comprehensive Schooling is Better and Fairer', *Forum*, Vol. 30, No. 2, Spring 1988.

on attainment of social class' – in other words, a
significant tendency for the average attainment of
the three levels of the 'manual working class'
(skilled, partly skilled *and* unskilled) to rise more
rapidly than that of the professional and 'intermediate' classes. These two trends the authors call
respectively 'improvement' and 'equalisation'.

For fuller information of this crucially important
study the reader is referred to the articles in which
the authors report their findings. However the key
diagram relating the changes in attainment by
social class origin over time is reprinted here as
Figure 1. Attainments are presented in terms of the
Scottish examination results (Higher and O-grades)
of each of the three cohorts studied (1976, 1980,
1984). While the historically and socially
determined sharp class differences still persist, the
recent (and sudden) trend towards equalisation is
clearly apparent. Obviously the scope for improvement is greatest among the working class, deprived,
as these children have been both north and south of
the Border, of any genuine access to science,
knowledge and culture. It is, therefore, only to be
expected that, once access is broadened, as the
comprehensive school allows, it will be precisely
these classes that improve their exam performance
most rapidly (without, however, holding back the
most advanced – or privileged). The expectation that
this would be the result was certainly one which
powered the comprehensive school movement originally – at least in the minds of its pioneers.

The authors hold that, although the 'equalisation'
trend is still small, it would be wrong to dismiss it as
trivial.

A political and historical perspective is essential

here. The Scottish system of selective post-primary schooling that was finally ousted in the 1970s had been configured well before the First World War. [The same could be said of the English system, B.S.] It subsequently reinforced social-class differences in attainment by shaping expectations both in local communities, and, in the national 'policy community' of administrators, school inspectors and leading teachers. The eight years that separate our early and late cohorts was but a brief period in which to unpick the legacy of decades.

Conclusions are clearly stated. 'Comprehensive reorganisation has helped to make schooling better and fairer in the past decade, and could do more in these directions.' Current government policies, however, 'are likely to retard and reverse the recent equalising trend'. Why this is so will be discussed in the next three chapters.

A final word here. In England and Wales, the researchers argue, the two Scottish trends are likely to be reflected, but to a lesser extent. Why? Because south of the Border there is more selection and creaming, 'fewer "all-through" (eleven to eighteen) comprehensives, and proportionately fewer communities that are served by wholly comprehensive systems'. But, they add, 'This does not mean that the potential for effective reform is any less than in Scotland.' What is required is serious, well designed research evaluating this whole development and its impact over time. 'Because there is no such study', they conclude, *there is little basis in research evidence 'for the widespread pessimism over the potential of comprehensive schooling outside Scotland'* (my emphasis, B.S.). This statement is perfectly fair and true. If this pessimism is widespread it is not derived from any objective knowledge as to what exactly is going on in these schools; a main source has been the headlines in the tabloid press and the loaded presentation of data in so-called 'quality' papers (like the *Daily Telegraph*) which should know better.

## 5 The Basis of Tory Policy

It may be, given the evidence quoted in Section 3 concerning consistent public support as well as academic achievement, that it is the very success of comprehensive secondary schooling – as opposed to the myth of 'failure' – that has contributed to accelerating the clear and energetic thrust of both the present government and DES officials to greatly enhanced central control – and now more recently to 'radical' plans aimed at circumventing, and destabilising, local 'systems'. Comprehensive secondary education, by its very form and structure, is potentially a great deal more open-ended than the functionally designed school system of the past to which, it is now clear, there can be no return. It is not only that a whole series of actions (and statements) first by Joseph and now by Baker and Thatcher reflect this new centralist thrust (particularly *vis-à-vis* local authorities and teachers) – a move that, as we shall see (Chapter 5) is encapsulated throughout the Education Bill – it is also that there has been for some time clear indications of a firm resolve on the part of senior DES officials to gain a tight control over schools and local school systems, with the object of bringing about a basic restructuring of education. The aim, it is now clear, is to ensure that things do not get out of hand in terms of preservation of the status quo, and particularly of ensuring social stability.

On this latter issue, a research study published in

1984 cast an unusually revealing light on the thinking of senior officials at the DES. After making it clear to the researcher, who was studying the relation between central and local government, that the central focus for the Department of Education and Science 'must be on the strategic questions of the content, shape and purpose of the whole educational system', adding 'and absolutely central to that is the curriculum' in relation to which 'we would like legislative powers', the anonymous high official interviewed gave expression to further concerns. Centralised powers were needed to cope with the dangers arising from over-education in a contracting labour market. 'There has to be selection.' the mandarin is quoted as saying, 'because we are beginning to create aspirations which society cannot match.' There follows an interesting admission.

> *In some ways this points to the success of education in contrast to the public mythology which has been created.* When young people drop off the education production line and cannot find work at all, or work which meets their abilities and expectations, then we are only creating frustration with perhaps disturbing social consequences. We have to select: to ration the educational opportunities so that society can cope with the output of education. (My emphasis, B.S.)

The arrogation of centralised powers, in defiance of traditional 'partnership' systems, has then a clear social purpose:

> We are in a period of considerable social change. There may be social unrest, but we can cope with the Toxteths. But if we have a highly educated and idle population we may possibly anticipate more serious

social conflict. *People must be educated once more to know their place.* (My emphasis, B.S.)[11]

The conclusion the study's author (Stewart Ranson) derives from this (and other) evidence is that 'The state is developing modes of control in education which permit closer scrutiny and direction of the social order.'

This, of course, is no new thing in the history of education; indeed involvement by the state in the restructuring and control of education for social and political purposes has been apparent at least from the middle of the last century. What is new are the modes of control that have rapidly been developed over the last three or four years, now culminating in the 147 clauses of the Education Bill. Significantly, the state, instead of working through and with other social organisations (specifically local authorities and teachers' organisations) is now very clearly seeking a more direct and unitary system of control than has ever been thought politic – or even politically possible – in the past. Thatcher's third victory has changed all that. Now all seems possible to those who feel they have, or feel as if they have, the ball at their feet.

There are basically two policies which could be pursued by any government at the present time. These are diametrically opposed. The first is simple and straightforward. It is to encourage and strengthen the existing system of comprehensive secondary education; to purge it of current weaknesses, to allocate adequate resources to allow development, to encourage local and school-based initiatives, and, above all, to re-establish an effective partnership with the local authorities (where also there are weaknesses requiring amendment), with the churches and all other concerned voluntary bodies, with the teachers and their organisations, and with parents and theirs. There needs also to be an energetic thrust to construct a complete system of tertiary education for all (see Chapter 6). This may be considered a tall order, and there would certainly be much to be done; but within such a policy a great deal might be achieved.

The opposite policy is that now pursued by the present government. This is to attempt to restructure the system by the creation of new types of school (such as the proposed city technology colleges and others) subject to market forces and designed to meet the needs of the yuppie and other intermediate strata; deliberately to destabilise and downgrade local authorities and their systems of comprehensive secondary education, similarly to downgrade the teachers' organisations, refusing them any serious involvement in developing the system, shouldering aside all other 'partners' (such as the churches) in a thrust for totally centralised control, with the final aim of establishing the three types or levels of schooling designed for different social strata outlined in Thatcher's interviews, quoted at the start of this chapter.

These two policies are stark alternatives. The central decisions are now to be made. In the following four chapters a full analysis will be made of this second alternative, now before the nation. We will return to a fuller discussion of the first alternative in the final chapter of this book.

### Notes and References

1 Marjorie Cruickshank, *Church and State in English Education* (London 1963), Chapter 7.
2 For instance, Julienne Ford, *Social Class and the Comprehensive School* (London 1969).

3 Christopher Jencks *et al, Inequality: A Reassessment of the Effect of Family and Schooling in America* (New York 1972); James Coleman *et al., Equality of Education Opportunity* (Washington 1966).

4 This scheme was originally announced as the answer to problems of the poor in inner cities, but the financial assistance has in fact mostly gone to relatively impoverished members of the professional classes. See J. Fitz, Tony Edwards and G.J. Whitty, 'Beneficiaries, Benefits and Costs: an Investigation of the Assisted Places Scheme', *Research Papers in Education*, Vol.1, No.3, 1986.

5 Gallup polls at that time reflected popular disgust with Tory policies. Answering the question 'Which party has the best policies to deal with education and schools?' in April 1986, only 16 per cent chose the Conservatives, 46 per cent Labour (16 per cent chose the Alliance; there were 22 per cent 'don't knows'). This was the lowest point reached in support for the Tories in a steady decline over the previous two years. (*TES*, 20 March 1987)

6 *Education Statistics for the United Kingdom, 1986* (London HMSO).

7 On a television programme shortly after the Solihull decision, Keith Joseph produced his now notorious statement of intent regarding inner school differentiation: 'If it be so, as it is, that selection between schools is largely out, then I emphasise that *there must be differentiation within schools.*' (*TES*, 17 February 1984)

8 The enquiry, entitled *Attitudes to School: a Study of Parents and Third Year Pupils*, was carried through in the summer of 1985 by the ILEA Research and Statistics Branch. The headline derived from the finding that 19 per cent of those surveyed in 1985 said that they 'were not really satisfied' with their child's school, compared to only 10 per cent in 1983.

9 The journalist responsible for reporting this poll was one Michael Durham ('Education Correspondent'). The fuller report on another page says that nearly one parent in five (18 per cent) is dissatisfied with their children's education at state school '*although 78 per cent are content*' (my italics, B.S.); presumably 4 per cent 'didn't know', but we are not told. On this page the story starts by saying that the poll (of 1,028 parents) '*indicates a high level of concern* over state education, with *many* believing standards have dropped in recent years' (my italics, B.S.). If Conservatives base policies on reporting of this character there is little wonder these are so often wide of the mark.

10 The article giving a full report of the research by Andrew McPherson and J. Douglas Willans is summarised by them in 'Comprehensive Schooling is Better and Fairer', *Forum*, Vol. 30, No.2, Spring 1988. Their original paper appeared in *Sociology*, November 1987, 'Equalisation and Improvement: Some Effects of Comprehensive Reorganisation in Scotland'.

11 These quotations are taken from Stewart Ranson, 'Towards a Tertiary Tripartism; New Codes of Social Control and the 17+', in Patricia Broadfoot (ed.), *Selection, Certification and Control* (London 1984), pp. 224, 238, 241.

# 2 Destabilising the Local Authorities: Open Enrolment and Opting Out

## 1 An Interrelated Strategy

The main proposals concerning schools embodied in the Education Bill were outlined in the set of 'consultation papers' mostly published (in inadequate numbers) at the end of July – responses being demanded within two months. In spite of protests from almost every organisation that responded, this timetable was rigidly adhered to; nor was there any indication that the consultation process would shift the government on any of the key issues; and this was borne out when the Bill was published in November. The proposals in the consultation papers which, unlike the Bill itself, attempt a rationale of the proposals in comprehensible language may, therefore, be taken as representing the main thrust of government policy. One set of papers concerned proposals for structural change – these are discussed in this chapter. Yet further proposals, relating to the Inner London Education Authority, and to further and higher education, are considered in Chapter 3. Proposals concerning curriculum and testing, embodied in the so-called 'Red Book' (actually another consultation paper) form the subject matter of Chapter 4.

The consultation papers relating to structure

covered four main areas: financial delegation to schools, open entry, charges for school activities and opting out ('grant maintained schools'). Considered separately, there may be something to be said for some of these measures (for instance, financial delegation to heads and governors). But considered as a set of interrelated measures, as they must be, each can be seen to provide its specific thrust towards the desired objectives – those of destabilising locally controlled 'systems' and, concomitantly, pushing the whole structure of schooling towards a degree, at least, of privatisation, so establishing a base which could be further exploited later. There is no doubt that the combined effect of these measures would mean the break up of the public system of education as we have known it since 1944.

There is, first, the proposal (clauses 23 to 36 of the Bill) to devolve financial responsibility for running individual schools (all secondary schools and all primary schools with more than 200 pupils) more or less completely to the governors (and, presumably, through the governors, to head teachers, though this is only mentioned in terms of the need to give heads 'appropriate training'). Some experience, though limited in scope (and leading to much contention) has already been gained, under existing legislation, in Cambridgeshire and elsewhere. There are a large number of problems here, such as overburdening heads (who will surely have to *do* the job) with financial management (was it proposed, asked Ted Heath, following the Queen's speech in June, to recruit 31,500 bursars?). But, of course, the main objective of this proposition is clear enough. It is to loosen the schools from the hands of the local authorities, and so encourage them (or some of them) to take the first step towards more advanced forms of independence.

Second, there, is the proposal (clauses 17 to 22) to allow 'open enrolment' (within a very broad limit) to all schools. Local authorities, in order to plan the contraction of their systems (due to falling rolls) in a rational manner, with the aim of maximising the effectiveness of the system as a whole in terms of equalising opportunities, have had powers until now to fix a limit to each school's intake. It is this which is to go. Schools, it is argued, must have the right to admit as many pupils as parents wish to send them, and so be permitted to expand considerably (and suddenly) – opening their doors also to pupils from other, nearby local authority areas. Unpopular schools, conversely, must go to the wall – and be closed as a result of the operation of this form of market forces.

The full implications of this proposal will be discussed shortly. In terms of overall strategy, however, the meaning of this step is clear. Popular schools, now with more or less full financial responsibility, will soon begin to differentiate themselves from the others. This provides the springboard for the next step – opting out – also provided for in the Bill.

Third, the Bill will include clauses (proposed as amendments by the government) legitimising the charging of fees by schools for certain activities. This was, of course, the issue where Thatcher put her foot in it during the election campaign, when she said that the objective was to charge fees in publicly maintained schools, only to be corrected by Baker. But fees for 'extras' seem a different thing – if, in fact, basically similar. The 1944 Act says that 'No fees shall be charged in respect of the education provision in any maintained school.' The intention, as outlined in the consultation paper on this issue (not published until October) is to modify this clause, and to permit such fees for 'extras' (for instance, visits to residential field centres, swimming baths, the theatre) to be charged. But today many schools (in more affluent areas) do make charges covering essential materials and equipment and the clear danger is that such charges will also be legitimised by the Bill.

In some local authority areas, charges covering essential materials are already permitted. But to legalise the process through a new statute is an entirely different matter. Clearly this fits into the general strategy very precisely. Popular schools in affluent areas will be permitted to charge such fees, as will others of course; but this will provide such schools with the opportunity further to differentiate themselves from the ordinary run of schools, and to some extent to narrow their clientele to the more affluent section of the local population. So now such schools are poised for break-out.

This takes us directly to the most important of the Bill's clauses (37 to 78) – those concerned with 'opting out', on which a consultation paper was also issued. This starts by claiming that the proposal is a response 'to the numerous indications it [the government, B.S.?] has received that groups of parents want the responsibility of running their schools as individual institutions'. The definition of the adjective 'numerous' in the Concise Oxford Dictionary is 'comprising many units' – or 'coming from many individuals' (as in 'the numerous voice of the people' – no doubt Baker's 'ordinary people'). The Secretary of State, when challenged (by parental organisations) has not, so far, been prepared to name a single one of these groups, or even units.

The proposal is that schools that wish to, or, more precisely, where governing bodies and parents wish to, may apply to 'opt out' from the local system of which they are a part, and become 'grant maintained' schools, receiving funds by direct grant from the DES instead of the local authority. By this means, all formal relations with the local authority would be broken. The school would become 'semi-independent' financed directly by the state. Hence Thatcher's contradictory phrase – these would be 'state independent schools'. A further direct effect would be that the local system, as a 'system' would also be broken. The main rationale for this drastic (radical?) step given in the consultation paper – apart from the perceived clamour of the people – is that this proposal 'will add a new and powerful dimension to the ability of parents to exercise choice within the publicly provided sector of education'. The greater diversity of provision which will result, it is added, should also 'enhance the prospect of improving educational standards *in all schools*' (my emphasis, B.S.).

As this is a matter of crucial importance to the whole future of the education system of this country, a more detailed analysis of this proposal, embodied in the Bill's clauses, will be made. The proposal applies to *all* secondary schools and to primary schools with more than 300 pupils.

The main proposition as set out in the relevant consultation paper, and now embodied in the Bill, can be put briefly. First, a school's governing body, at a single meeting, by means of a 'simple majority', may resolve to opt out (and apply to the Secretary of State for grant maintained status), informing the local authority of the decision. This proposal must, however, then be referred to parents with pupils at the school. The parents' decision would be determined, once again, by a 'simple majority of those voting'. Thereafter there is a procedure of consultation, the Secretary of State having the power of final decision. The proposed legislation has additional features concerning such applications in specific cases, but these are not of immediate importance except in one case. If governing bodies do not themselves take the original initiative, parents are to be encouraged 'to express their view' independently. This could be done by their circulating a proposal which, if it secured the support of a number of parents 'at least equal to a fifth' of pupils at the school, 'would oblige the governors to hold a secret postal ballot'. A 'simple majority' of voters favouring opting out would *require* the governors to activate the necessary procedure. (A quick calculation indicates that, if pupils have two parents, a group consisting of one tenth of all parents could set this procedure in train.)

In the late autumn a sharp difference of view between Thatcher and Baker on the extent to which it was expected that opting out would be taken up surfaced. Thatcher received wide publicity for her statement that she expected and hoped that the great majority of schools would opt out. Immediately after – perhaps more conscious of the fears and growing opposition to this measure within the educational world – Baker said that only very few schools were expected to take this option, though later he modified this by saying he expected very many to opt out 'by the mid-1990s'. However that may be, the consultation paper, emanating from Baker's office (the DES), specifically states that the government intends 'to assist the creation' of an 'association or trust' independent of the DES, but having the specific function 'to promote the development of grant maintained schools', act as a centre of advice to their governing bodies and also 'in due course' take on 'some administrative functions'. The intention is clearly to use the power of the state to encourage their development, and indeed, in September, Baker announced in this connection that 'he would launch a drive to persuade parents to "opt out" of local authority schools' (*TES*, 25 September 1987).

Several other points could be made, but this analysis must be brief. First, no school would be permitted to 'opt back' until ten years after the initial decision. Second, parents with children transferring to a school considering opting out in the next year or two have no vote, while those of pupils about to leave do. Third, foundation or 'first' governors of 'opted out' schools would hold office for from five to seven years; governors elected later would hold the post for only four years; members of the governing body of ex-county (local authority) schools would apparently be chosen by that governing body itself (that is the governing body would be self-perpetuating). Finally it is stated in the consultation paper that 'it is the Secretary of State's intention' that opting out schools 'should retain their previous character', e.g. a comprehensive would remain comprehensive, a grammar as a grammar (and presumably, though as usual ignored, a secondary modern would remain such). A school wishing to change its character would be required to publish statutory proposals, allow comment, etc. This, of course, refers to the possibility of a total change (from comprehensive to grammar, for instance); it does not pertain to what might be called 'creeping change' resulting from increased selectivity in relation to 'ability', class, race or gender – a matter returned to later.

The clauses concerning opting out are quite certainly the most important part of the entire Bill in terms of structural change. Their immediate – and longer term – implications are considered below. But the focus here is on the thrust of this entire interrelated set of measures: financial delegation, open entry, legalisation of fees for certain activities, and finally opting out. Because it seems clear enough (and indeed has been frankly stated by Thatcher) that there is a further aim which goes beyond anything proposed in this Bill. This would be a bid for 'independence' by successful opted out ('grant maintained') schools; that is, their recruitment to the independent sector. This could be achieved through a combination of fee-paying by parents (who will anyway be increasingly paying for 'extras') and direct support from the Treasury through a large extension of the Assisted Places Scheme, by which fees of 'selected' individual pupils are paid directly by the DES. Many independent schools already rely on this source of funds for their very existence – it seems probable that several were saved from bankruptcy when the measure was introduced in the early 1980s. There has already been talk of just such an extension of the scheme. By this means, the objective of increasing the provision of purely 'independent' schools for the middle strata, at the expense of the publicly provided system of schooling, becomes a practical possibility. It is an additional irony that the project will, of course, be financed by public money dispensed by a department of state.

Nothing has so far been said about the twenty or more 'city technology colleges' which the government intends to establish, relying particularly on funds extracted (reluctantly) from industry. The first of these to attempt to recruit pupils is at Solihull (the favourite Tory authority) where the project met sharp resistance from the adjacent Labour-controlled authority of Birmingham, which does not wish to see disruption of an orderly recruitment to its local comprehensive schools. The second is planned for Nottingham. Clause 80 of the Bill provides for the establishment of such 'colleges' (actually schools), giving the Secretary of State powers to make 'any payments' in respect of both capital and current expenditure incurred. The contribution from industry could, therefore, be minimal (until now industry was supposed to contribute the whole capital cost), nor is any limit laid down on the number of such schools. No consultation paper was issued on this issue, nor has there ever been any opportunity for effective public discussion of this initiative, and its implications. The open-ended commitment written into the Bill again indicates the determination of the government to bring into being the 'variety' of semi-independent schools Baker favours, at the expense of disrupting local systems. These colleges will have the further effect, should they attract pupils, of ensuring the re-introduction of selection at the age of eleven with its inevitable backlash within primary schools (the Solihull City Technology College is developing a whole series of what sound like exceedingly amateur 'tests' for this purpose).[1]

So the Tory strategy for the schools becomes clear. If the Education Bill goes through, each of Thatcher's three grades of school will be provided for, though development of the picture will take time. The independent sector will be enhanced by recruitment of 'successful' opted out schools, in the manner indicated earlier (and no doubt also by further budgetary measures to ease the viability of private provision); a whole set of 'grant maintained' or 'state independent' schools will have been prised out of local authority control and, together with the city technology colleges (and the like) will form a confused and somewhat anarchic 'system' for the middle strata primarily subject to market forces. At the bottom will be what is left of today's local authority systems, consisting largely of a set of 'financially devolved' schools run by governing bodies, continuously threatened by further opting out of schools, but in fact catering for the mass of Baker's 'ordinary people'. This hardly seems a recipe for stability, even if it accords with the Tory image of an educational system adapted to, or matched by, a structured, hierarchical society.

## 2 'Consultation' and the Response

With the issue of the consultation papers in July it became clear that the main thrust of government policy was embodied in the two related papers – on 'open entry' and 'opting out' (entitled 'open enrolment' and 'grant maintained schools'). In spite of the problems of the summer months (August and September), hundreds and even thousands of missives reached the DES by early October – and these covered the entire spectrum of organisations concerned directly with the schools. On 'opting out' these, according to press reports, expressed unanimous hostility.

'Overwhelming condemnation of the government proposals to allow schools to apply to opt out of local authority control has come from education officers, teachers, local government and all the larger organisations of parents,' reported the *Times*

*Educational Supplement* (2 October 1987). 'It is now clear', the report added, 'that Mr Kenneth Baker will face unprecedented hostility from educational professionals if he presses ahead without significant amendments to his opting-out legislation.'

Through the autumn months there was, however, no sign of any 'significant amendments' being conceded, and this in spite of urgent, face-to-face, personal pleas by the main organisations directly concerned with running local systems – the local authorities. These have two associations. The Association of Metropolitan Authorities (AMA) represents the main urban centres throughout the country and is now, as traditionally, Labour dominated. The Association of County Councils (ACC) consists largely of shire counties and, although traditionally Conservative dominated, was in 1987 'politically hung'; the Tories, who control twenty-five of the local education authorities concerned, are the largest single group but are now outnumbered by Labour and Alliance – having a newly elected Labour chair of the Education Committee (Mr Fred Newell of Notinghamshire). While the AMA directly opposed opting out (and other proposals) the ACC voted more narrowly against late in September, (by twenty-three to eighteen), although the Conservative minority had clear reservations on this issue (*TES*, 2 October 1987).

Representatives of both these bodies met Kenneth Baker at the end of September, when the ACC was reported as 'fiercely critical' of the financial delegation proposals. At this meeting Baker (according to the *Guardian*, 1 October 1987) 'offered to work with Labour controlled local authorities to make sure his proposed programme of sweeping reforms succeeds in practice'. But nothing seems to have come of this. At a further meeting, on 21 October, Baker 'bluntly refused to alter his radical reform plans for English and Welsh schools' in the face of what is described as 'sharp criticism and serious misgivings from local authority leaders *across the political spectrum*' (my emphasis, B.S.). He made it plain to leaders of the AMA and ACC 'that the four main planks of his Bill ... would not be altered whatever critics said'. Most of the local authority leaders 'left the meeting empty-handed and angry'. One declared that it had been 'a dialogue of the deaf'. Neil Fletcher (chair of the AMA Education Committee) complained that they had spent two hours at the DES 'trying to be reasonable and helpful', but we got 'absolutely nothing in response'. Clearly, he concluded, Baker was 'no longer master in this building' – the agenda 'is being set by 10 Downing Street' (*Guardian*, 22 October 1987). It will be remembered that Thatcher characterised the Education Bill with the poll tax as 'flagship' legislation; and that she chairs the Cabinet committee on the Bill.

Towards the end of September, before the fruitless encounter just described, the AMA and ACC, sinking some political differences, took a joint initiative and set up a Standing Conference on Education, together with representatives of teachers' and parents' organisations, the Institute of Directors, the Trades Union Congress and the Anglican, Roman Catholic and Methodist churches. The aim was to 'attempt to find a broad-based collective voice' in response to the government's projects 'in a climate of growing opposition to the proposals' (*TES*, 25 September 1987). The initial conference of this organisation – attended by 180 representatives from 60 organisations – took place in Birmingham on 26 October. Described as 'historic' by the *Times Educational Supplement*, the conference expressed virtual unanimity on all the main issues.

It is quite clear, then, that instructions had gone out (from the 'flagship' presumably) that *no* concessions were to be made. Pleas for the extension of the 'consultation' period were rejected out of hand[2] and a firm stand taken on the measures outlined in the original papers. To these we may now turn. Although I have argued earlier that these need to be considered in their interrelations, in order to examine the detailed and precise significance of each, they will be taken in turn, together with the criticisms of responsible educationists.

## 3 Open Enrolment

The main problem with this proposal is that 'open enrolment', in the form proposed, will disrupt local authority planning and thus render nugatory their responsibility to ensure equality of conditions in schools comprising local 'systems'. The point has been clearly made by Peter Wilby, education editor of the *Independent*:

> Under the 1980 Act local authorities are required to set an annual intake for each secondary school. Until that limit is reached, they are obliged to admit any child whose parents apply for a place. The intake level is not necessarily the same as a school's physical capacity. Many authorities set the admissions limit automatically low to ensure that all their schools get a fair share of pupils.

Until now, the argument continues 'authorities have

not been able to set the limit more than 20 per cent
below a school's intake in 1979, without reference to
the Secretary of State'. The proposed legislation,
however, requires that 'Admission limits must return
to the 1979 levels, when pupil numbers throughout
the country were at their peak'.

Wilby then gives a good and clear example as to
how and why some authorities 'have openly
manipulated admissions limits to ensure that the
quality of education in relatively unpopular schools
does not suffer' – to allow, by contrast, 'free rein to
market forces' would 'reduce opportunities for some
children and, in the end, create less parental choice'.
Suppose you have three comprehensives (as at
Coventry),

> each with space for 1,000 children, but only 2,400
> children in the locality. If two schools are allowed to
> recruit to maximum capacity, the third, unpopular
> school (probably on the local council estate) is left
> with only 400 children. Unless the authority
> commits disproportionate resources, that school will
> get fewer teachers, less money and fewer subject
> options.

If the 'popular' schools are then permitted further to
extend, for instance by adding new buildings (as
both Baker and Thatcher have hinted may be the
strategy) then 'the unpopular school would close,
leaving parents with a choice of two schools, not
three' (*Independent*, 14 May 1987).[3]

Another relevant example comes from
Oxfordshire. Tim Brighouse, the Chief Education
Officer, writes:

> In Witney ... Oxfordshire County Council was able
> to share out a temporary fall in student numbers
> between two schools, a former grammar and

secondary modern respectively. The ex-grammar school was sometimes (wrongly) perceived by the public to have the better academic reputation. In fact both schools were equally successful academically.

Had the 1986 Act not existed, one of these perfectly good schools might have been crippled by innuendo and rumours and would have required massive and expensive public subsidy to maintain it. (There were too many pupils to amalgamate the two.) The other school would have become painfully overcrowded. As it was, each school prospered. The now expanding town needs two good schools and has two good ones. (*Independent*, 25 August 1987)

Brighouse concludes: 'By encouraging open enrolment, the government will diminish parental choice in the end.'

It is this, and more especially the need for rational planning – particularly at a period of rapidly declining school rolls – that is profoundly disturbing to those who have the welfare of the educational system at heart. 'Open enrolment', states an editorial in the *Times Educational Supplement*, 'means the negation of planning':

Anybody ... responsible for more than one school serving a single area, would be bound to make plans about catchment areas and pupil numbers if they wanted to use their physical plant and human resources to the best advantage. That is to say, they would be bound to intervene – to apply human intelligence to the achievement of the best results, rather than leave it to the free and unfettered operation of a quasi-market.

But leave it to the market is what they will now have to do, continues this editorial. 'Planning will, in future, be retrospective; a matter of picking up the bits and presiding over the bankruptcies after the

consumers have made their educational purchases.'
The proposal, as it stands, 'is going to raise costs and
lower efficiency' (*TES*, 17 July 1987).

It is hardly surprising that, in their responses to
the consultation paper, all those organisations
directly concerned with the school system were
unanimous in their hostility to the proposal for 'open
enrolment'. Existing arrangements, said the AMA,
allow LEAs (the local education authorities) 'to
manage falling rolls sensibly and carry out schemes
of reorganisation with minimum disruption'. The
new proposal, on the other hand, 'puts in jeopardy
the community use of school premises', places too
great an emphasis on buildings (in terms of
accommodation) 'and none at all on staffing or
curricular balance', and takes no account of
'providing a variety of school places, with convenient
access, properly planned class sizes and decently
maintained premises'. Mr Bob Morris, the AMA's
education officer, is quoted as saying: 'This
free-for-all will do educational damage and will in
the end impoverish parental choice.' (*TES*, 3 July
1987) The ACC argues that unplanned growth can
affect the quality of a given school, that parents may
be led to expect 'a greater freedom of choice than can
be delivered', and that the proposal generally will
lead to 'overcrowding and poorer standards'; this is
taken from a summary of responses to DES
consultation papers, issued by the Standing Conference for Education (SCE) at its Birmingham
meeting on 26 October 1987.

What of parents' organisations? These surely
might be expected to support Baker's proposal if, as
he claims, it is tailored to increase parental choice.
In fact, their unanimous view is one of unremitting
hostility. The National Confederation of Parent

Teacher Associations (NCPTA), uniting over 4,000,000 parents, states firmly that if more choice were to be 'a reality for all parents irrespective of where they live and what their income is' the confederation might be inclined to welcome the policy. But the proposals advanced 'will not bring this about'. For one thing 'popular' does not necessarily mean 'good' and 'good schools' might be destroyed 'by ill-founded comment'. The NCPTA standpoint is clearly stated.

> Parents essentially want to be able to send their children to the local school ... and want to be confident that the educational opportunities available in that local school will be such as will bring out the best in their children in whatever direction their talents may lie.

The Campaign for the Advancement of State Education (CASE) a long established organisation uniting parents and teachers in the defence of publicly provided education, is also very clear in its approach. The 1980 Act, with its provision for appeals and other measures, 'gives a good balance between the rights of the individual and the needs of all children in an area'. In 1979-80 the schools were very full 'and parents hoped falling numbers would give better standards of space'. In any case what is proposed 'is a very blunt instrument'. CASE does 'not think this proposal will lead to more choice. By forcing less good schools to close, it will reduce effective choice.' Children would be best protected against false choices through 'the present balance between individual rights and local planning' (SCE).

Similar reservations come from the Advisory Centre for Education (ACE), a consumer organisation concerned particularly to offer parents a consultancy service. Open enrolment, ACE believes, 'would reduce and not enhance, choice for the majority of parents and children'. Since 'choice' became a buzzword the centre has had an increase in calls from 'disappointed parents'. ACE then faces up to a crucial issue.

> Unless certain guarantees can be built into this legislation to ensure that children in both 'popular' and 'unpopular' schools receive a full curriculum, adequate staffing and resourcing and stability, then open enrolment will singularly fail to deliver extended choice. (SCE)

Finally the National Association of Governors and Managers – which includes many lay people and also parents – has produced a highly ambivalent response, to say the least. 'Popular' schools may well get overcrowded so that valuable new uses of space (for information technology, for instance) may have to go by the board. In any case the association would like to see a great deal more co-operation between schools, rather than the present tendency to work in isolation. 'Proposals that set schools in competition with one another will make this more difficult.' Nor is 'the most popular school' necessarily 'the one which provides the best all round education' (SCE).

Administrators are hostile – how can they plan? Parents are hostile, calling for proper resources for local schools. What of the teachers? Heads of secondary schools will, of course, be those most directly affected. These are united, with deputy heads, in the Secondary Heads Association (SHA), consisting largely of comprehensive heads but also some from independent schools. This body has been the most outspokenly hostile of any organisation.

Current proposals are 'astonishing, contradicting everything the government has said in *Providing for Quality* [an official document], and ignoring the work of the Audit Commission'.[4] Head teachers do not believe the system will work, they continue, but can see that 'it will cause endless expense and lead to the most undesirable results'. The contraction of the service 'must be planned and rational, not whimsical', and the SHA *'is unremittingly opposed to all the proposals in this paper'* (my emphasis, B.S.). Particularly feared are 'the effects of choice being made on racial grounds' (SCE).

The National Association of Head Teachers (NAHT), with some 27,000 members, largely unites the heads of primary schools, who will also be directly affected by the proposal. Here again the attitude is one of total opposition. 'The government's proposals for securing wider parental choice will create an inefficient system which will raise parental expectations which cannot be met.' Inefficiencies are bound to result from a system of market forces which will make it very difficult for LEAs to manage pupil numbers economically, and the need to keep open under-subscribed schools for geographical or social reasons or simply because 'popular' schools are turning pupils away. Parental expectations cannot be met since more schools will have to close than under the present system, thereby reducing choice, and over-subscribed schools will have to turn pupils away when filled, so disappointing many parents. It is the firm conclusion of the NAHT that *'LEAs must continue to have reserve powers to plan efficiently and effectively on educational grounds.'*

The three other main teachers' organisations take a similar stand. Referring to the presently prevailing system of admission limits to schools as rolls fall, the Assistant Masters and Mistresses Association (AMMA) which has 114,000 members, largely comprehensive and grammar school teachers, insists that 'the government's reversal of its own policy' in this respect 'will make it virtually impossible for LEAs to manage resources efficiently in the interests of the pupil population for which they must provide'. The AMMA 'regards the proposals as damaging and in the long term likely to restrict rather than increase choice for all pupils' (SCE).

This view is paralleled by that of the main teachers' organisation in England and Wales, the National Union of Teachers (NUT), with 201,000 members. The proposal, while appearing 'superficially attractive', will have 'profound and damaging consequences for the provision of education in each LEA'. A whole series of reasons are given to support this view which must unfortunately be omitted for lack of space. Among reasons for the total opposition expressed by the NUT's sister organisation, the National Association of Schoolmasters and Union of Women Teachers (NAS/UWT), with 101,000 members, are these. First, open enrolment will place an extra burden on an authority 'which is responsible for providing a broadly based curriculum for *all* pupils in *all* schools within its area'. Second, an over-subscribed school 'will have to resort to selection which is contrary to the philosophy of comprehensive schools'. Third, teacher morale will suffer because of the redeployment or dismissals likely. The proposal is described as '*a malicious attempt by the government to drive a wedge between LEAs and governing bodies*' (my emphasis, B.S.) – in the name of 'parental choice'.

Generally speaking, then, the teachers' organisations take up very much the same position on open enrolment as do organisations speaking for local authorities, parents and governors.[5] They are uniformly hostile. This stand is also reflected by organisations representing the labour movement. In the view of the Trades Union Congress, to give 'free rein' to parental choice, as proposed, 'will widen divisions between schools, and seriously reduce educational opportunities for some children'. LEAs will be 'unable to plan their education provision' to 'ensure viability of all the schools in their areas'. All this will have 'disruptive effects' on both staff and children – effects which have been overlooked (SCE). This view is seconded by the National Association of Local Government Officers (NALGO), a major union representing staff employed in schools, colleges and LEA central education departments. Open admission, the union claims, subverts the role of LEAs in planning, threatens their ability to maintain a range of different forms of school and represents, in fact, the negation of LEA powers 'to ensure appropriate provision for *all* children' by a complete disregard for the future of those schools adversely affected by opening up admissions procedures to market forces (SCE).

Finally, it is symptomatic, and of general interest, that perhaps the strongest of all statements on open enrolment comes from the Church of England. In October the Bishop of London, Dr Leonard, chair of its Board of Education, forwarding to Mr Baker individual responses to each of the consultation papers, also addressed to him an open letter relating to 'the whole package of proposals relating to schools'. This letter (to be looked at in more detail in Chapter 5) specifically stresses the need to ensure that scarce resources are made available with 'a basic fairness'. 'We believe', writes Dr Leonard speaking for the church on educational policy, 'that this applies also to physical resources which is why we cannot support an entirely "open" admissions system.' The untrammelled operation of market forces 'is not appropriate to the provision of a public good'. And the point is driven home with something of a hammer blow, by one of the more conservatively inclined of bishops. 'Creeping privatisation of the education system is no more acceptable than would be the outright handing over of all schools to commercial enterprises.' (SCE)

Also opposed to the proposal is the Methodist Church which points to 'unplanned consequences' and the effect on 'reduced' schools in terms of staff morale, resources, LEA inability to manage the teaching force and consequently the curriculum.

It would be tedious to cite at length from other responses – by the independent educational journal *Forum*, PRISE (Programme for Reform of Secondary Education), the National Association of Primary Education and others. All stress the same central points; disruption of local planning, the fate of 'unpopular' schools, reduction not extension of choice – except for parents with cars who can whizz kids to distant schools or manoeuvre the decisions of governing bodies or a local parents' group. What emerges from this survey is that, on a central issue of Thatcher policy cunningly presented, people who know about educational organisation and administration and the needs of those who work in and use the schools are not to be misled. That is why Mr Baker frames a populist appeal to 'ordinary people' urging that no one should attend to the 'educational establishment' to which he has no respectable answer. What he seeks to obscure and ignore is the fact that parents' organisations, teachers, local authorities, school governors, trade unions immediately concerned, and the various churches are entirely united in their opposition to his proposed measure. In the consensus view that has clearly emerged, the policy he seeks to force on the nation would *operate to disrupt and destabilise a school system* which opinion polls have shown is in fact very acceptable to the great majority of parents.

### 4 Opting Out (Grant Maintained Schools)

There is no doubt whatever that the central focus of the Thatcher/Baker proposals, in terms of structural change, are those concerned with 'opting out' ('grant maintained schools'). This has been very clearly seen by all those responding to the consultation papers, as will appear. There is a 'strong' and a 'weak' version of these proposals, as we have already noted. Thatcher intends that the great majority of schools eligible will take up the option. Baker has publicly stated that only a few are likely to 'opt out'. But in this case why does his paper on the subject announce the intention to establish an official body specifically to encourage 'opting out'? An intention, as we have seen, later specifically emphasised by Baker personally.

It is on this issue that Lord Whitelaw is on record as saying that the government may expect particular difficulties in carrying the proposed legislation through the House of Lords, many members of which have a close and expert knowledge of and concern with education. Why should there be such concern about the implications of this particular proposal?

The Tory election manifesto first aired the proposal to legislate for 'opting out'. It was immediately submitted to a devastating critique by

Tessa Blackstone, then Deputy Education Officer (Resources) of the Inner London Education Authority.[6] This proposal, she concluded, while at first sight having a populist appeal for parents promised a ballot, would actually mean that:

> Schools will be torn apart by conflict between those who want to stay and those who want to leave the LEAs. Staff rooms will be divided. Parents will be lobbied on all sides and left confused and divided.

The whole system, she predicts, will be destabilised. Children 'will be caught in the middle and the job of educating them neglected while the battle rages'. No wonder head teachers had rejected the idea as 'beyond belief'. Opted out schools would be cut off from the LEA, left without back-up services, without support for curriculum reform and innovation, without advice on school welfare benefits such as uniform grants and free school meals. 'Where will the children in difficulties go who need home tuition?' – a service currently provided by LEAs. 'What will happen to the links LEAs have built up between primary and secondary schools to ensure continuity for pupils, as schools opt out on a random basis?' As for Baker's claim that schools can be financed on the basis of average per capita costs, this 'is a recipe for financial chaos'. Children's futures, Tessa Blackstone concludes, are now 'threatened by a scheme casually destructive of the best in the maintained system, dangerously divisive and administratively unworkable' (*Guardian*, 9 June 1987).

The fact that opting out is not likely to be a liberating, but a profoundly conservative force, has been underlined by Anne Sofer, SDP spokesperson on education.

> The most basic and primitive motive any group of
> people ... has for acting collectively is in self-defence.
> The one thing that can be guaranteed to start up the
> whole campaigning rigmarole is a perceived threat
> to the status quo. Grammar schools, for which
> comprehensive reorganisation is planned, schools
> facing a tertiary college reorganisation, any school
> with falling rolls threatened with amalgamation, all
> of these will be able to mobilise effectively to make a
> bid to opt out. Already most of the few schools that
> are quoted in the press as talking about the
> possibility fall into this category. (*TES*, 17 July
> 1987)

An example here, incidentally is Silverdale in
Sheffield, a 'successful' comprehensive, which the
authority wishes to reorganise, as part of a tertiary
system (*TES*, 2 October 1987).

Tessa Blackstone's criticisms, which rightly focus
on the likely effect on children and teachers, as well
as those of Anne Sofer, have now been reiterated
time and again by responsible educationists and
indeed by virtually every organisation concerned
with schools. The 'overwhelming opposition' from
'education officers, teachers, local government
organisations and all the larger parents' organisations', reported in the *Times Educational Supplement* (2 October 1987) has already been
referred to, as also the fact that no concession
whatever had been made on this issue.

Those most directly (and personally) affected are,
of course, the Chief Education Officers responsible
to the Local Education Committees for running
systems of schools. Their organisation, the Society of
Education Officers (SEO), argues strongly that
opting out 'will delay and seriously affect the
rationalisation of schools, currently faced with
falling rolls, and inhibit the efficient use of scarce

resources'. (In this connection the controller of the Audit Commission, an official body monitoring local government expenditure, is reported to have said that opting out 'could threaten savings of between £500 and £700 million' – owing to the impossibility of rational reorganisation.)[7] The SEO is also concerned that no provision is made for consulting school staff, nor parents at local primary schools 'whose children are likely to be affected'. Further criticism focusses on the fairness of the proposals. Grant maintained (opted out) schools 'will control their own admissions entirely and they will be able to be selective', said David Nice who drew up the SEO response. 'They will be able to select the most able pupils, the best motivated pupils, the pupils from the most affluent families who will be in a position to produce the biggest financial contributions,' he went on. 'There will not be parity of esteem, or parity of pupils' ability or motivation.' They will be selective, and, referring to the effect on the schools left with the authority, by this 'unilateral' action 'they will turn the LEA schools into secondary modern schools'.

The SEO develop a number of other 'wounding criticisms' of the opting out proposals. Parents will have no right of appeal if their children are refused a grant maintained school place; there will be no external scrutiny of governors' decisions on admissions; there will be increased transport costs, particularly in rural areas. Equally important, the lack of accountability by opted out schools could make them prey to political hijacking. 'These schools will control large sums of public money, but they won't be accountable to any elected body.' The governing bodies which, as we have seen, will be self-perpetuating 'could be taken over by political parties and could become party political schools', Mr Nice is reported as saying (*TES*, 2 October 1987).

'We cannot find any merit in them,' is the concluding statement of the Society of Education Officers passing judgment on the proposals of a Secretary of State. That opinion, reported the *Times Educational Supplement* (2 October 1987) 'is shared by almost all the main educational groupings'.[8] The unanimity among all these organisations has been very striking – a hostility even more strongly evident on this issue than on open enrolment. Let us look at the main responses, once more considering each main grouping in turn.

To begin with the local authority associations, the Association of Metropolitan Authorities describes the proposed procedure as unsatisfactory and says the criteria for assessing applications (vested in the Secretary of State) are unclear. Staff in opted out schools will be isolated while transfer arrangements are inadequate. Links between primary and secondary schools will be disturbed; there will be no proper control or monitoring of such schools while, above all, 'The coherent and comprehensive planning of education provision in an LEA area would be undermined.' No attempt has been made to quantify the demand for opting out – the AMA 'suspects the government is out to create the demand'. There will be a tendency towards creeping selectivity. Schools should not 'be able to pick and choose the best pupils and leave the rest to the responsibility of the local authority'. But the fundamental issue, said Neil Fletcher, chair of the AMA education committee, 'is whether schools should belong to the whole community and be accountable to its elected representative or be put in the hands of a small, transient clique of activist parents' (SCE).

The AMA may be Labour dominated while the Association of County Councils is 'hung', but the latter is also openly hostile. The proposals 'while increasing the autonomy of relatively small groups of parents in some areas, would reduce the economy, efficiency and effectiveness of the provision of education for the population as a whole'. In the event of reorganisation proposals, the opting out of a school threatened with closure would mean the closure of another 'possibly more popular school'. That school is then likely to apply to opt out 'as a defensive measure', and this could go on, school by school, 'throughout the whole area'. The effect would be (as predicted in the opening section of this chapter) 'the creation of a new sector of independent schools funded by tax- and rate-payers with little public accountability' (SCE).

The main parental organisations express strong opposition – even if it is in the name of enhancing 'parental choice' that the proposals are legitimised. The National Confederation of Parent-Teacher Associations (NCPTA) 'firmly rejects' the proposals, saying that, 'They will in themselves do little to bring about the stated objectives,' adding that 'there is no evidence' of 'large numbers of groups of parents who wish to run their own schools'. All that is needed to make schools more responsive to parental wishes is to strengthen the powers of governing bodies by laying a duty on them to obtain parental support for the curriculum – as a safeguard against the introduction of what the NCPTA regards as unsuitable material.

'We totally oppose these proposals,' reports the Advisory Centre for Education, the consumer organisation, describing 'grant maintained schools' as 'clearly a cover for the reintroduction of selection in one form or another'. This outright opposition is 'as much from concern for the opted out schools themselves, as for the way that whole communities will be affected by decisions that can be taken by an unrepresentative minority of transient parents'. Opting out 'spells planning blight, unequal representation of parents on governing bodies, selection, and unequal opportunities' (SEC).

The government's proposals are 'dictatorial, divisive and racially inflammatory', says the Campaign for the Advancement of State Education. As for grant maintained schools, 'We totally oppose this scheme.' First, local accountability, via locally elected members, is essential. Second, the schools are ours in trust. It is 'morally wrong' that one generation of governors and parents 'should be able to remove from community control schools which past generations have worked and paid for, and future generations look to'. A vote by a majority of a group of parents could be 'quite unrepresentative'. Further, opted out schools would face an uncertain future – a school 'succeeds' through the living interests of its parents, staff and community, not vague 'local worthies' (of whom governing bodies would be composed). It is particularly shocking that schools which opt out should be permitted to appoint unqualified staff. Finally CASE warns (like others) of the dangers of 'racial tension and ultimately apartheid' (SCE).

Who will the governing bodies of opted out schools be responsible to? A pertinent question from the Association of Governors and Managers. What say will the local community have – if schools are to be the direct responsibility of the Secretary of State? As for the decision being left with a simple majority of current parents, these may by no means reflect the much wider interest in the community's investment in a school (SCE).

The same informed criticism comes from teachers. There is no evidence of a widespread desire by parents to take on the running of schools, affirms the National Association of Head Teachers, 'nor does the government provide any'. It appears unconcerned about 'the extremely adverse' effect the proposal would have on local authority reorganisation plans, 'many of which have been prepared at the instigation of the DES or the Audit Commission'. The NAHT is at a loss to understand how opting out could improve standards in schools remaining with LEAs, and by what means the measure will 'widen parental choice for the overwhelming majority of parents' (SCE).

Serious dangers are discerned by the Secondary Heads Association in proposals which 'will not improve good schools, but will certainly weaken those that are less strong'. Governors of grant maintained schools 'are likely to be narrowly interested in the interests of their own school, and the broad educational needs of the whole community' may very well be 'neglected'. Procedures for opting out are unsatisfactory, while staff in the schools concerned 'might be treated very badly'. Without rejecting proposals out of hand the SHA sees moves to force through legislation in the autumn of 1987 as 'hasty and ill advised' (SCE).

There is uncompromising but well informed criticism from the largest teachers' organisations, whose members represent the great majority of those teaching in publicly maintained schools. The proposals 'are intended to cater for an articulate, privileged elite', declares the National Union of Teachers. They will certainly not enhance choice for the majority of parents and children. What has been issued is 'a spurious and false appeal to concepts of parental choice and raising standards, which will do nothing in practice to improve the quality of education for all, but will prove to be damaging and divisive for the education service' (SCE). The NUT also holds that opted out schools 'will not accept children with special educational needs', either because they will want to give their schools an elite character, or because they will have cut themselves off from essential LEA support services. Organisations concerned with children with special educational needs, for instance, the Voluntary Council for Handicapped Children, have voiced strong opposition, and great concern. 'Quite frankly I think the government has forgotten about children with special needs in the proposals,' commented the council's chair. 'If they are there at all it is as an afterthought.' (*TES*, 23 October 1987) At a conference of the Greater London Association for Disabled People the mood was reported as 'angry and confused'. Opting out schools would reject such children – the proposed legislation was seen as setting back progress towards integration. And generally, the question has been raised as to how, in the new dispensation, can a *coherent* local authority policy for integration be devised, and realised?

Schools should not be allowed 'to apply to the Secretary of State to be funded direct by central government', says the National Association of Schoolmasters and Union of Women Teachers. Besides fragmenting the maintained sector this would mean recruitment to opted out schools reflecting 'a philosophy and ethos that are hostile to state schools', render LEAs incapable of planning rationally for contraction, mark a further step towards dismantling the public education system, reintroduce selection and result in a general increase in costs. Even the 'no strike' Professional Association of Teachers (PAT) can only manage a muted support since it voices strong objections to specific aspects of the proposals; notably the 'simple majority' proposal; the non-involvement of 'professionals' in the decision to opt out; the need to allow for opting back to LEA control (SCE).

It is heartening that trade unions show a close knowledge of and interest in the problems of organisation and administration. Reiterating criticisms voiced by others, the TUC foresees a move to 'a two tier education system'. With the blocking of rationalisation plans there will inevitably be mounting costs. In the absence of adequate training and resources the laying of responsibilities on governors is 'a recipe for educational and financial chaos'. And what about continued community use of schools? Here is a key point hitherto not mentioned, and the TUC is also concerned about diseconomies of scale and arrangements for specialist advice to grant maintained schools. NALGO has declared the union to be 'completely opposed' to proposals which can only be 'damaging and divisive to the service as a whole'. It is particularly concerned about 'the iniquitous position in which LEAs will be left – funding schools outside their control, statutory duties without power or funds to carry them out, and increased costs for providing their own services' (SCE).

Finally – the churches. A particular paragraph in the open letter by Dr Leonard of the Education Board of the Church of England advances 'some major reservations'. The introduction of grant maintained status could lead to the creation not just of 'an alternative system' thereby increasing parental choice, but of 'a privileged sector' established at the expense of the rest of the system and thereby actually decreasing the extent of significant choice open to large numbers of parents.

It is quite clear, the letter continues, 'that the effect of large scale adoption of grant maintained status will weaken the position of local government in a fundamental way' (SCE). These are perceptive points and indisputably correct, echoing criticisms from the bulk of educational organisations – though the haste imposed by the 'consultation' process meant that each organisation responded on its own.[9]

Warnings put forward in various submissions are being borne out already in the case of some schools planning to opt out as soon as may be. Two cases in point are Ongar in Essex (which the LEA plans to close as part of a reorganisation plan) and Silverdale in Sheffield (whose sixth form would be lost as part of a necessary tertiary reorganisation plan covering the whole city) (*Guardian*, 3 August 1987; *TES*, 2 October 1987). Kingdown School in Wiltshire, a successful comprehensive, plans to take the same road, seeing this as necessary to self-preservation, even though the head has declared himself ideologically and professionally totally opposed to the scheme (*Observer*, 11 October 1987). It is no wonder that there is a very serious concern about this whole move among Conservatives, as expressed by the Conservative Education Association, as well as by leading Members of Parliament, notably Ted Heath, Leon Brittan and John Biffen, and by some members of local authorities; this is an aspect we will take up in Chapter 6. Meanwhile it is worth noting that late in September, under the heading

'Hasty Reform of Education', the *Financial Times* devoted a main leader to the issue. Recalling Thatcher's vocal support for 'wholesale opting out', and her expressed desire that 'these newly independent schools' should become 'more selective', the leader stresses the world of difference there is between the establishment of a few 'magnet schools', and a 'wholesale creaming off by thrusting middle-class parents'. This policy 'might damage the most vulnerable children by leaving them in sink schools'. Opting out, it is concluded, 'is only a part-market system, which might be more destructive than none at all'. The British government has yet to show 'signs that it has thought deeply enough' about its Education Reform Bill. It is by no means only about opting out that 'further thought is required' (*FT*, 22 September 1987).

As the weeks have passed no evidence has come to light that the slightest further thought has been given. On the contrary, the clauses in the Bill itself show the government pig-headedly determined to carry through its original proposals unchanged – whatever the views of those most closely concerned.

## 5  Financial Delegation and Charges for Extras
### (i) Local financial management

Financial delegation and charging for 'extras' are, perhaps, less controversial than other proposals, though severe warnings have been given about the possible impact of both sets of measures. Their crucial role as an element in the general thrust of government policy has already been indicated but here we may review opinions expressed in responses to the consultation papers.

Generally speaking, most organisations support

the concept of local financial management 'in principle' but are extremely critical of the actual proposals made in the official consultation paper, calling for considerable modification and, in several cases, a less hasty approach to this whole issue. The government has adopted a 'big bang' approach which could result in chaos, says the Association of Metropolitan Authorities. It is seeking 'to go too far too fast'. School-based managers may not be best placed for making decisions on resource management. Major problems will arise in determining how to allocate sums of money to schools in ways that take account of social needs. (There has tended to be a degree of positive discrimination in this matter on the part of local authorities with an overview of the scene.[10]) Major items of repair and maintenance will inevitably pose problems, not to mention a whole range of LEA activities overlooked by the government paper – home and hospital tuition, peripatetic teaching, teachers' centres, the entire career service. Particular difficulties may arise in relation to community facilities on a school campus. Above all – and here is a point many others reiterate – local authorities will be deprived of the power to appoint staff (although in the case of heads and deputies they *must* proffer advice – a later 'concession' written into the Bill) and to redeploy staff in the (certain) event of falling rolls. The scheme as a whole (and this point is very strongly pressed by the Audit Commission[11]) will cost more to administer.

These doubts and warnings reflect the concerns of most of the main respondents. The Association of County Councils, for instance, regards the staffing proposals as 'impracticable, expensive and inefficient'; the position of LEAs as employers responsible for health and safety legislation might well prove untenable (SCE). Parents' organisations, while favourable in principle, find fault with various aspects of the proposals. CASE thoroughly objects to giving governors sole responsibility for appointing staff – 'The ratepayers pay much of the cost and should be represented.' ACE is very doubtful if many parents will volunteer as governors, given the enormous responsibilities to be imposed – for staff management, health and safety, appointments and finance – unless they have 'the support of a real partnership with the LEAs'; a point strongly underlined, it is interesting to note, by the National Association of Governors and Managers, the body best able to assess the significance of the proposition. Governors will need support, says NAGAM, training, compensation for financial loss, including loss of earnings, if the job is to be done effectively.

Teachers' organisations raise similar points. Management systems have yet to be 'successfully tested', argues the Assistant Masters and Mistresses Association, expressing total opposition to the proposals; nor are school staffing levels in any way adequate to discharge a host of new responsibilities. Even where teachers accept the principle of delegation they have criticisms to register on the basis of specialist knowledge and concur in condemning attempts to move 'too far too quickly' in the words of the AMA. Finally the TUC is in line with several others in stressing the very real problems involved, and calling for pilot studies to be 'established and evaluated' before there is any talk of full scale development of powers and duties.

As has been demonstrated, the main objective of this measure is to distance schools from local authorities and generally deprive these of powers. The attack on local government as a whole is one of

Thatcher's clearest objectives. A key stage in this whole process, to be set in motion by Baker's Bill, is financial delegation which must be speedily allowed for alongside 'opting out' and 'open enrolment' to realise the aim of creating a new category of 'state independent schools' under *centralised* control. September 1989 is the deadline set by Baker for the implementation of this proposal. Here is the reason for the unseemly haste shown in pressing ahead with this aspect of the total policy.

## (ii) Fees for 'extras'

There remains one consultation paper in this category – on the issue of charging for certain aspects of schooling or 'educational extras' which, as we have seen, is a central feature of the government's set of interrelated measures. As this paper was issued very late, few responses are to hand from organisations at the time of writing, though there has been one major response from Professor Richard Pring of Exeter University who has consistently defended the publicly provided service against creeping privatisation (*TES*, 23 October 1987).

The proposition to charge for whatever may be designated as 'extras' was first aired in the Queen's speech at the end of June, to meet with immediate objection. If there is going to be a public education system 'which divides young people according to their parents' ability to pay', said James Hammond, deputy general secretary of NCPTA, on behalf of parents, it will mean that those who cannot pay will have a lower quality education: 'We will fight, might and main, to prevent that happening.' (*Independent*, 25 June 1987) The teachers' view came from the

deputy secretary of the NUT, Doug McAvoy, that the
school curriculum must be broad, including non-
academic subjects and sport. 'All of these are
essential parts of the curriculum and all must be
free.' In other words there could be no charging for
such aspects as 'musical instruction and field trips'
without undermining equality of access to a broad
curriculum. The point was underlined by the former
Labour Shadow Minister for Education, Giles
Radice, when he suggested that, from now on,
'Parents can expect an end-of-term bill to go with
their children's end-of-term reports.' Those who can
afford to pay will get 'sports, music, field trips, and
more for their children. Those who cannot won't.'
That would be the outcome if the term 'extras' was
applied to any 'vital part of school life' which 'should
be available to all' (*Independent*, 25 June 1987).

Doubts resurfaced with the delayed appearance of
Baker's consultation paper. Announced early in July
as due 'almost immediately' (*TES*, 3 July 1987), it
was not in fact isued until 1 October. That it failed to
tackle several of the key issues was immediately
pointed to by the *Independent*. What, specifically, is
meant by the free provision of an 'adequate' supply
of books, was one question. Many parents are
already making substantial contributions to their
children's school funds, commented Simon Midgley,
and the present proposals 'could further legitimise
this practice'. The whole trend of the government's
thinking was in this direction, commented Neil
Fletcher, of the AMA's Education Committee,
towards forcing local authorities 'to raise more and
more by charging for services that have hitherto
been provided for the general good of the community'. Payment for 'extras' was 'the first step on
the slippery slope to fee paying' in the nation's

schools, added Jack Straw, now Labour's Shadow Education Minister (*Independent*, 3 October 1987).[12]

It is worth noting, incidentally, that the closing date for responses to this consultation paper, allowing only eight weeks for organisations to reply, was 30 November – *after* the date on which the Bill was scheduled for publication. This is how things worked out; the original Bill contained nothing on this issue, which was left to be dealt with as an amendment by the government to its own Bill. There was a serious miscalculation here in the matter of timing, as in so many other things.

'The government remains firmly committed to the principle of free school education', the opening phrase of the consultation paper, is cited by Richard Pring who places the whole issue in context in 'Free to Those who Contribute' (*TES*, 23 October 1987). What, precisely, does this mean – which services should or should not be paid for, how much should parents be expected to contribute? A government that can seriously contemplate privatisation of the prison service, he suggests, is 'less "firmly committed" ' to principle 'than it cares publicly to admit'.

Although official pronouncements relating to education exclude the term 'privatisation', the relevant and now easily recognisable advance measures are already in train in various ways – in line with thinking 'deeply rooted in government, especially Treasury' circles as to the need to privatise public services generally. Study of this issue, argues Pring, clearly shows a general shift from the free education of the 1944 Act to an education dependent primarily for its quality on private means. First, public money has been allotted to private schools (through gradual extension of the Assisted Places Scheme and through tax and rate incentives); second, private support is expected for public provision through parental contributions for lessons, books and materials, together with a search for covenants and sponsors; third, cuts in financial allocation have impoverished the maintained sector leading to a choice by parents either to buy private schooling for their children or dig deeper into their pockets to ameliorate poor conditions in the local school they attend.

A recent survey of conditions in one LEA by the Campaign for the Advancement of State Education is cited. This 'revealed a woeful tale of inadequate resourcing, teacher-time devoted to money-raising rather than teaching, and poorly maintained buildings that at times were deemed dangerous'. Recent figures also reveal that the publicly provided system is falling dramatically behind fee-paying private schools in the provision of books (private boarding schools spend almost three times the average for local secondary schools).[13] Year after year reports of Her Majesty's Inspectors on LEA expenditure policy 'demonstrate the unsatisfactory resourcing of our schools'.

Pring argues that there is evidence and to spare that the value of the government's verbal commitment to 'free education' – for 'adequate' provision of basic requirements – depends entirely on its definition of 'adequate' for children who remain in public sector schools. And this 'appears to be very much less than what teachers and parents may think'. The commitment to 'free education', then, must be treated with caution. It must be spelt out in terms of ensuring acceptable standards of maintenance of premises and in the provision of resources; especially in relation to 'the central core of the curriculum'. Especially to be protected from any charges are provision 'in the arts, in residential experience, in field trips, in physical education, and in the many activities which teachers and parents see to be essential to the improvement of standards'. Provision of these aspects should not necessarily follow current LEA practices which differ radically one from the other. The commitment must be to meet the needs of *all* children according to age, ability and aptitude.

This chapter has dealt with the main structural – or administrative – 'reforms' in the Education Bill. It is absolutely clear that, if carried in the form presented in the clauses of the Bill, these would certainly destroy the system of education that now exists in this country. It must also be clear that, far from a 'reform' Bill, this is quite easily the most reactionary piece of legislation on education ever to have been presented to Parliament and people. Edward Heath has described it as a 'confidence trick', and so it is. But what we have dealt with so far is only part of an outrageously extended measure.

## *Notes and References*

1 For a critical evaluation of this initiative, see Clyde Chitty, 'The Commodification of Education', *Forum*, Vol. 29, No. 3, Summer 1987. Later information confirms that the Solihull entry was selective, there being 316 applicants for 180 places. The three-stage selection process involved an interview, a 'reasoning' (or 'intelligence') test, and a primary school report.

2 Baker's letter to the AMA, which had asked for an extension until December, contained a clear refusal to extend the deadlines. But, he added, 'Consultation does not end with the expiry of the deadlines on each document. The continuing public debate over the coming months will valuably inform Parliament's consideration of the Bill.' (*TES*, 2 October 1987)

3 See Andy Stillman and Karen Maychell, *Choosing Schools* (NFER 1986) from which this example is taken.

4 The Audit Commission is an official body that monitors local government expenditure.

5  A fifth organisation, the Professional Association of Teachers, seems
   ambivalent in their response, but warns that an admissions policy
   determined only by market forces would be 'not only ineffectual but
   dangerous'. The education of the nation's children 'is too important
   to be regarded simply as a commodity' (SCE).

6  Now Master of Birkbeck College, London University, and a Labour
   peer, Tessa Blackstone was earlier Professor of Educational
   Administration at the Institute of Education, London University.

7  The Audit Commission's point, as reported, is that local authorities
   will not propose schools for closure if they fear they will opt out –
   some authorities, they say, have already suspended rationalisation
   plans for this reason. The government's 'reforms', will, therefore,
   'perpetuate wasteful distribution of resources' (*TES*, 16 October
   1987).

8  The *TES* report continues, 'Only one, the Hillgate group of radical
   right thinkers (widely seen as having been the main influence in the
   opting out plan), has come out positively in its favour.' The full
   signifance of opting out has been well brought out by Sir Roy
   Harding, General Secretary of the Society of Education Officers and
   a distinguished ex-CEO himself, in 'Careering off Down the Wrong
   Road', *TES*, 3 July 1987, and by Howard Glennerster, Professor of
   Social Administration at the London School of Economics, in
   'Goodbye Mr Chips', *New Society*, 9 October 1987.

9  The Roman Catholic church is also totally opposed to opting out and
   is mobilising political support against the proposal (*Independent*, 11
   November 1987). The Methodists do not object in principle, but have
   a number of specific criticisms (SCE).

10 The original proposal was that schools would be allotted a sum of
   money based on a formula relating to pupil ages. This would not
   have allowed for any differentiation in the level of funding between
   schools. In an attempt to meet widespread criticism of this plan,
   Baker reluctantly committed himself (verbally), late in November, to
   consider allowing extra financial help to 'unpopular' schools – those
   losing pupils, therefore funds, and so caught in a downward spiral
   (*Independent*, 30 November 1987). Some saw this as first evidence of
   relaxation over the market forces policy.

11 The Audit Commission has warned that this measure was likely to
   lead to duplication and higher administrative costs – citing both
   Cambridgeshire and Solihull (pilot authorities) as cases in point
   (*Guardian*, 9 October 1987).

12 A recent survey in Hertfordshire, claimed Jack Straw, showed some
   secondary schools raising thirty-three times as much money through
   charging as poorer schools. Among primary schools the difference
   was fourteen to one (*Guardian*, 3 October 1987).

13 Figures from the Educational Publishers' Council, referring to 1986.

# 3   Further Depredations

Before turning to more fundamental issues concerning schools we need to look, however very briefly, at two further areas covered by the Education Bill – proposals to break up the Inner London Education Authority, and those concerning further and higher education.

## 1   Breaking up the ILEA

First, it is necessary to be clear about what is a rather complicated situation in the capital city. London has had a unitary education authority for 117 years, ever since the election of the first School Board following the Education Act of 1870. The responsibilities of the London School Board were then passed to the new education committee established under the next Education Act of 1902 (or, in London, a special Act of 1903) as happened in all counties at that time. Subsequently, in 1972, when there was local government reorganisation, the London County Council became the Greater London Council which also had its education committee responsible for London education. The GLC did much for London but the Tory government abolished it in 1985, in the teeth of a popular campaign to preserve a unified approach. But one

victory was won, the setting up of a directly elected
education authority (the only one in the country)
with full responsibility for all aspects of the publicly
provided education facilities in London. This is the
Inner London Education Authority (ILEA) which
has continued to preserve the experience of a single,
unitary education authority which has prevailed for
over a century. Certainly the largest authority in
England, this is the heir to an immense experience
of administering education in the nation's capital
city.

The ILEA covers thirteen boroughs (counting in
the City of London which is strictly not one).[1] It does
not include all the boroughs in the metropolitan
area, some of which have been in the news because
of 'radical' policies, which lie around the periphery –
Brent, Haringey and Ealing, for instance. At one
extreme are well heeled Barnet and Harrow, at the
other the very disadvantaged Newham. The government's proposals for the break-up of the ILEA have
nothing to do with these outer London boroughs.

It was in 1936 that Labour first won control of the
London County Council and in the post-war 1940s it
became the pioneering authority in developing
comprehensive schools, launching an ambitious
'London School Plan' already in 1944. But there
have since been enormous demographic, or
population changes including the concentration of a
high degree of disadvantage, poverty and immi-
gration. Nearly half ILEA pupils now qualify for free
meals – the best indicator of relative disadvantage.
More than one-fifth have unemployed parents. A
quarter of London's pupils speak a language other
than English at home – as many as 160 different
languages are represented. In addition, many of the
pupils live in some of the worst housing in Britain.

The very existence, first of the LCC then of the GLC often under Labour control (and challengingly situated in full view of Parliament directly across the river) was frequently a thorn in the flesh of Tory governments, particularly lately. The GLC, as we know, was finally abolished in 1985 and the current attempt is, in fact, the fifth to abolish the ILEA (or its predecessors) in the last decade (*TES*, 23 October 1987). Until now, on each occasion it has emerged unscathed, and the NUT in its response to the Consultation Papers on this issue, quotes positive statements by both Mark Carlisle and Keith Joseph. 'The nature, scale and importance of the education service in Inner London', Joseph told the House of Commons in 1984, 'justify a directly elected authority in this special case.' Kenneth Baker, ironically, is also on record robustly defending the ILEA. To allow individual boroughs to opt out, he argued in 1980, would leave 'a rump of poorer deprived boroughs' and would increase the administrative expenses of running inner London's education. It is now precisely this that he himself proposes to do.

The consultation paper starts by dismissing the ILEA as a failure in two brief assertions.

> There was severe criticism of the ILEA on the grounds of its educational performance despite levels of expenditure far in excess of those of any other LEAs in the country ... But the new ILEA has shown little sign that it is ready to tackle the root causes of its educational and financial problems.

Current proposals are then set out. Briefly these allow individual boroughs to 'opt out' of the ILEA at any time and run their own education. The opting out decision may be made by a simple majority vote at any one council meeting – no consultation is necessary either with parents and governors, or with the teaching and non-teaching staff. Only one month is permitted for local people to lodge objections with the Secretary of State, in whose hands the final decision rests. There is a provision allowing boroughs to opt out jointly – probably to cover the City of London which could not possibly run a system of education. Teachers in opting out boroughs are to be transferred as a block to the new authority, while all present ILEA assets within the boundary of the opted out borough are to be transferred. The document provides no clear solution as to what is to happen to advisory, peripatetic and supply teachers, but it seems that these would in general remain in the employ of the ILEA; there is a similar vagueness as to the future of the central staff. Finally a complex section on finance argues that the proposed unified business rate will ensure that boroughs staying with the ILEA will not be adversely affected, while it is expected that the ILEA will make 'commensurate savings'. Opted out boroughs are to take over in 1990, when the poll tax is planned for implementation. The Education Bill does, however, include one clause (115) not foreseen in the consultation paper. This is to the effect that, if eight or more boroughs decide to opt out, the Secretary of State may dissolve the ILEA and require the remaining boroughs to run their own education.

It is crystal clear that these draconian measures are intended to render powerless, and indeed break up, the ILEA, leaving it (in spite of the new clause) with that 'rump' of severely disadvantaged boroughs inveighed against a few years ago by Baker himself. This is a vindictive act, and seen as such by many observers. Indeed the *Times Higher Education Supplement*, referring to the 'especially oppressive restrictions' Baker has placed on the ILEA in the area of higher education, interprets these as simply one aspect of the 'sordid vendetta' on which Baker is engaged. He is determined to break up the ILEA 'against all sense and against the wishes of the overwhelming majority of parents', the editor writes, 'so here anything goes' in what is described as 'the dirty war Mr Baker is waging against the ILEA' (*THES*, 31 July 1987).

Much of the criticism of the ILEA has been politically motivated and, as the NUT says, 'intended to undermine the credibility of the authority'. While there have certainly been examples of inefficiency, in fact the most recent analyses have found that, if social and economic factors are taken into account, academic results in ILEA are equivalent to the average for the country as a whole – on a par, for instance, with Oxfordshire and substantially above some outer London boroughs such as Bromley. Costs, of course, are bound to be substantially higher in London than elsewhere. In many areas, on the other hand, ILEA educational achievements are substantial. These are effectively set out in the NUT response, and the reader is directed to this source for a full statement of the situation.[2] These cover not only the schools, but also the generous facilities for further and higher education and especially for part-time adult education, where present provision accounts for as much as 25 per cent of all adult education in England and Wales. Indeed in many ways the ILEA has led local authorities generally in activities which have been of exemplary value to the country as a whole. Its research and statistics unit is

nationally and internationally known, as are many
of its products, the latest being the largest and most
comprehensive research study of junior school
children ever carried through in this country.
(*School Matters: the junior years*). The ILEA also
recently commissioned the well known Hargreaves
Report (*Improving Secondary Schools*), the only
thorough and professional study of secondary
schools – their curriculum, inner structure and
processes – whose influence has spread throughout
the country, as well as the Thomas Report on
primary education and the Fish Report on integration of pupils with special needs, an area where
the ILEA has been engaged in much pioneering
work. Indeed, the ILEA has consistently played a
central, pioneering and innovatory role in the past
and continues to do so today. Its deliberate
destruction deeply dishonours the perpetrators.

There have, apparently, been over 3,000 responses to the government's consultation paper, the
great bulk of them from individuals, and (although
we are not, of course, told officially) almost
unanimously hostile to what is intended. No notice
whatever has been taken of these. In October,
William Stubbs, a highly respected public servant,
and Chief Education Officer to the ILEA, took the
unusual action of attempting to inject some
rationality into the proceedings by writing to the
*Guardian* to express his views, and plea for a serious
reconsideration of what was being proposed. The
letter, printed under the heading 'When ILEA is
Driven to Distraction', stresses the point that, 'No
one appears to be examining the implications of
these changes for the whole of the inner city.' Mr
Stubbs adds that, 'notwithstanding the best efforts
of those involved', the result of the proposals is likely

to be 'a breakdown in the administration of the service in the capital'. This, he went on, 'is no special pleading of a bureaucrat seeking to prevent improvements or defend territory'. What he is asking is that the Secretary of State should 'review more widely the education service in London rather than confine his attention to parts of the area' (since his concern is solely with the opting out boroughs, B.S.). 'I want', he told the *Times Educational Supplement*, 'everybody to reject the conclusion of the Secretary of State and look at the whole of education in Inner London.' (*TES*, 16 October 1987)

It will not now surprise readers of this book to learn that Kenneth Baker 'immediately turned [this proposal] down flat' (ibid.). Chaos for the children of the capital in the rush for political advantage is what appears to be the most favoured course. There is not space here to discuss the kinds of problems bound to arise should the present proposals go through Parliament unamended, but these are clear enough. All the consultative paper's proposals are given legislative form in the Education Bill itself. These clauses (114 to 125), together with the opting out clauses for schools, have been identified by Lord Whitelaw as at risk when they reach the House of Lords. It should not be too much to hope that, at the eleventh hour, there may be a reprieve at this point.

## 2  Further and Higher Education

The general theme which runs through the whole Bill – that of the denigration and downgrading of local government – remains the central factor of the government's radical, and many think ill thought out, proposals in the field of further and higher education as a whole. The whole of Part II of the Bill, including clauses 81 to 113, deals with this issue. This book deliberately focusses on the schools so no more can be done than provide a brief outline of the general proposals for higher education, and consider these in the light of responses by those particularly concerned. It should be said at the outset, however, that the proposed transformation of the system is of the greatest importance and deserves the closest public scrutiny and discussion.

In this area a number of steps, presaging legislation, had already been taken before the election. Several consultation papers, elaborating proposals made in a White Paper, *Higher Education: meeting the challenge*, published on 1 April 1987, were issued over the next two or three months. The first concerned the 'nationalisation' of the polytechnics and of other of the larger institutions of further education – that is, their removal from the control of the local authorities which originally nurtured them and their establishment as semi-independent corporations financed by central government through a new funding body, the Polytechnics and Colleges Funding Council, which would take the place of the existing National Advisory Body. The second document announced the proposed demise of the University Grants Committee and its replacement by a slimmed down 'Universities Funding Council' with substantial business representation. The third attempted to elaborate a new approach to funding by 'contracting' – described by the *Times Higher Education Supplement* as 'simply waffle' (*THES*, 15 May 1987). All these 'meagre documents', the *THES* continued, 'reveal the underlying shallowness, not to say triviality, of ministerial policy for higher education', generally regarded as a disaster area.

Matters took a new turn, however, after the election and the decision to give priority to the Education Bill. A further consultation paper was now issued specifically on 'Maintained Further Education', its 'financing governance and law'. The closing date for responses – 9 October – meant that once again, vitally important matters were to be determined with no more than a formal bow in the direction of democratic procedures. And in fact *all* the propositions in this paper, with only minor exceptions, reappear in clauses of the Bill, in spite of the highly critical attitudes taken by most of those concerned. 'A deeply cynical exercise', commented the National Association of Teachers in Further and Higher Education (NATFHE), this is simply another example of the consultation that never was.

The main thrust of this paper relates to the government's determination to 'steer' all further education colleges (including polytechnics) away from local authority and local community control towards development as institutions directly serving business interests. This is to be achieved by a two-pronged attack, which bears a close relation to proposals for the schools. First, the governing bodies of the colleges are to gain direct control of their own budgets, to have powers of 'virement', i.e. spending at will, and of hiring and firing all staff, including the Principal and Vice-Principal (though in these cases, local authorities must be 'consulted'). These responsibilities and duties are to be the province of the governing bodies of all institutions with more than 200 'FTE' (full-time equivalent) students – that is, all except the smallest. But the second prong of the attack relates precisely to this – the proposed composition of these governing bodies. At least half of these, it is proposed, should represent 'business, industrial, professional, and other employment interests' (including a small minority of trade unionists). On the other hand, in order that they should be seen to be 'properly independent' of local authorities, the latter's representatives 'would be limited to at most one-fifth'.

So, as well as taking over, lock, stock and barrel, huge capital assets in terms of buildings and equipment, local authority representatives are to be reduced 'at a stroke' to a small and therefore largely powerless minority on the governing bodies of 'their' institutions. Taking the 'model' given in the paper, of a total of twenty-four members, twelve would be employers and the like; four would represent the local authority. Other interested groups are likewise downgraded. Academic staff are to be allowed only two representatives, the thousands of students (many of them 'mature') only one. The original suggestion that two places should be reserved for 'parents' is not included in the Bill, while the proposal that only a representative of the 'employment interest' be eligible as chair of the governing body has been modified to allow local authority representatives also so to act. Given the importance of bolstering the position of governing bodies 'as an independent force clearly distinct from the LEA and the college', the consultative paper had argued, it would be 'inappropriate' for anyone from any category other than the 'employment interest' to do the job. The general intention could hardly be clearer!

This whole set of proposals has as its aim the transformation of the whole field of further education, including not only polytechnics and colleges of higher education, but also music, drama and art colleges – even adult education centres and

colleges focussing largely on initial teacher training
– into direct adjuncts of the local business world,
having a solely utilitiarian or instrumental direction. This, as might be expected, has met with a
chilly response, to say the least, from local
authorities (whose colleges they now are), from
academic and non-teaching staff within the colleges,
and from their own students who already have
undertaken a whole series of demonstrative actions
against them.

The Association of County Councils noted that the
consultative paper 'proposes new machinery to drive
the system', but 'denies the LEAs the tools to drive
the machinery effectively itself'. In some ways the
proposals seem designed to create between LEAs
and their colleges 'the sort of difficult relationship
that has in recent years been said to exist between
LEAs and central government'. The difference is
'that college governors are not accountable to an
electorate', and that LEAs' 'scope for any initiative
will be limited' (SCE). The ACC also casts doubt on
the ability of governors to find time and energy
effectively to carry out the heavy duties for which
they will be responsible, a point also strongly
underlined by the Association of Metropolitan
Authorities.

The National Union of Students has been severely
critical of the 'narrow instrumental view' of higher
education as expressed by all the government's
consultation and other papers on further and higher
education issued before the election. These see
higher education 'merely as a means to provide
qualified personnel for industry'. There are other
participants in the field of further education and
their needs have been ignored. Further, in the NUS
view, local authority control 'has been very

successful', particularly through 'integrated advanced and non-advanced provision geared towards local needs, and through increased access'. While accepting the need for strong links between higher education and industry, the NUS 'rejects the notion that this should be the primary concern of education'. The NUS view is, in fact, well thought out and cogently expressed (SCE).

This point is developed by other organisations, particularly those concerned with the schools, and with students below the age of nineteen. The Campaign for the Advancement of State Education, for instance, points out correctly that further education colleges include tertiary colleges, with students engaged in full-time study between the ages of sixteen and nineteen, as functional parts of local comprehensive systems. It is important, if such areas are to be properly cared for and safeguarded, that business interests (which are encouraged to be motivated by privatisation of the colleges' resources) do not dominate, but are balanced by parents and the wider community.

Indeed a whole number of implications arise when the proposals are considered from this angle. It is, for instance, remarkable (but in another sense unsurprising) that the consultative paper makes no mention of any form of tertiary organisation, and provides no clues as to how these might be accommodated in the proposed new dispensation. There is one statement that bears on this, referring to the need for planning and co-ordination 'both between colleges and in relation to neighbouring schools'; and in fact there has been much increased collaboration between colleges and schools recently relating especially to making effective provision for the sixteen to nineteen age group. In the Gadarene

rush to business control, however, all this is left out
of account, which bodes ill for the future, particularly if the colleges are to become semi-autonomous,
as proposed. Who is to plan and encourage this kind
of collaboration? In whose interest is it? In that of
the business 'community'? It is clear, as the *Forum*
response concludes, that 'the proposals would be
detrimental to tertiary planning'.

There is also the question of adult and community
education, currently provided in a variety of settings
including colleges of further education, community
colleges and schools. For a number of reasons this
important service has fragmented recently, and
reform is needed. But to delegate full financial
control to institutions whose prime function is the
provision of another kind of education is likely to
marginalise adult and community education, since
the perspective of a single institution is inevitably
narrower than that of an LEA accountable to the
whole community. The proposals are, therefore, also
likely to be detrimental to continuing adult and
community education as a community-wide service.

It is in fact impossible to characterise all work done
at colleges of further education as vocationally (or
business) oriented. Most colleges offer a wide range
of courses, some of recreational or personal interest.
The proposed composition of governing bodies is
likely to distort the balance in favour of employment
interests, and in disregard of wider community
interests. The consultation paper, concludes the
educational journal *Forum*, exposes 'considerable
misunderstanding by the government' of the
'complexity, flexibility and sensitivity' of further
education as it has evolved, and is consequently
'misconceived, mischievous and threadbare'. It
seems probable that, if these proposals are

implemented – and as mentioned earlier all feature in the Bill – enormous damage may be done to another important sector as well as to the schools – the field of further education.

The Education Bill also puts the final touches to the long prepared assault on the independence and (relative) autonomy of the universities. There are two main sets of clauses in the Bill which have this objective. The first (already mentioned) relate to the actual abolition of the University Grants Committee (UGC), which has traditionally acted as a 'buffer' between the state and the universities, but whose degree of independence has been thoroughly eroded in recent years. This is to be replaced by the 'Universities Funding Council' – a smaller body with fifteen members appointed by the Secretary of State. Of these six to nine are to come from higher education and the remainder from 'other backgrounds'. This body will no longer have the important function of advising the government on the development of the university system, and on the level of funding required. Its job is to act as a conveyor belt for government decisions – to administer the funds provided for the universities by the Secretary of State. These may be earmarked (allotted only for specific, defined purposes), both by the Secretary of State and by the Universities Funding Council in distributing them to individual universities. Once again, the whole arrangement allows for administration from the top downwards, leaving little scope for initiative by individual universities.

In this connection, as briefly mentioned earlier, the Bill also abolishes the National Advisory Body (NAB) which acts in parallel with the University Grants Committee, being responsible for 'public sector' institutions (polytechnics and larger colleges). The NAB has the job both of advising government on the overall level of finance required, and of distributing it to individual institutions. Unlike the UGC, local authorities, the TUC and academic staff (NATFHE representatives) are represented, so that discussion and decisions in this area are more open and democratic than in the case of the UGC, which has no such broad representation. The NAB has become increasingly unpopular with the government, due to its failure to do its bidding, and indeed its resistance to the official policy of closures, etc. It is, therefore, to be abolished. The new funding arrangements proposed for universities and colleges (including polytechnics) are clearly seen as providing transmission belts for policies determined in Whitehall.

The second set of clauses (130-134) relating specifically to universities proposes the abolition of tenure in university posts, long held to be the guarantee for full freedom of thought and expression among university teachers. This is to be abrogated through new statutes for each university to be drawn up by Commissioners appointed by the Secretary of State under the Bill (or Act). The amended statutes are to allow for dismissal of university academic staff on grounds of redundancy or financial exigency, and for 'inefficiency'. Although government representatives earlier indicated that a specific definition of 'academic freedom' would be written into the Bill, seen as vital by many in order to protect staff from wrongful or prejudiced dismissal as a result of views expressed or actions undertaken, no such definition figures in the Bill.

Deep concern has been expressed about the implications of these clauses, which, since they are tacked on at the end of the Bill and overshadowed by the far-reaching nature of the clauses concerning schools, are not likely to gain much Parliamentary time (particularly in the Commons). A main leader in the *Times Higher Educational Supplement*, whose editor, Peter Scott, has proved himself over a long period as a very knowledgeable commentator in the field of higher education, makes an acute analysis of the government's intentions across the whole field. Those behind the Bill as a whole 'are not benign'. Since the government deliberately chose to cover the whole field of education in one Bill (instead of two, one covering the schools, the other higher education), the plans for higher education must be seen 'in the context of its total strategy for educational reform'. University autonomy and local authority discretion 'are victims of the same oppressive drive to centralise power in the DES'. The failure to produce coherent plans for the sixteen to nineteen age group will have a profoundly adverse affect on higher education. The fact that there will be no statutory protection of academic freedom may prove disastrous. While the universities should certainly be encouraged to be more open and accountable, the means proposed in this Bill will hardly have that effect. The ill-named 'Education Reform Bill', unlike its 'genuine progenitors' will not stand 'the test of democratic scrutiny when more generous and civil-minded times return' (*THES*, 27 November 1987).

Ralf Dahrendorf, the widely experienced ex-Principal of the London School of Economics, is similarly deeply concerned. The Bill 'would give the Secretary of State explicit powers of direction which the governments of free countries ... usually try to dissipate or deny'. Government sanctions are to be introduced against universities and polytechnics. In what sense, Dahrendorf asked, have universities 'failed the nation', as government Ministers have been heard to say? Britain has 'a much envied system ... which has coped with the great expansion of access in an exemplary manner'. The combination of 'intensive undergraduate teaching and research related studies has ... worked well in Britain'. 'It has also been comparatively cheap.' Having had personal experience of several systems, Dahrendorf goes on, 'I would claim that the average British university costs roughly half as much as its Continental counterpart of the same size.' (*Independent*, 2 December 1987)

Dahrendorf questions the ability of Secretaries of State to handle the universities, or to know what to do with their many new powers. How effective will the people with 'capacity in industrial, commercial and financial matters' be – 'a new set of actors in higher education'? The Bill will be regarded as threatening by many academics 'not least because it removes safeguards of freedom which exist in all other countries of the free world'. 'By weakening institutional safeguards' this Bill 'exposes one important sector of British life to the benevolence, and by the same token to the possible malevolence, of those in power'. The government, he concludes, should think again.

Oddly, official support for much of what Ralf Dahrendorf is saying came, perhaps inadvertently, from a government representative only very recently. In the House of Lords on 25 November, Lord Glenarthur (who he?) advanced two propositions relating to higher education in a debate on overseas students (according to Lord Wedderburn, in a letter to the *Guardian*, 2 December 1987). First, 'British education remains among the best in the world.' Further, 'A British education is comparatively inexpensive when seen in the context of its quality.'

Despite a period of 'unprecedented financial restraint', Lord Wedderburn (Professor of Commercial Law at the London School of Economics) goes on, this statement confirms that British universities still give first class value, and have discharged 'to the full their duties of social accountability and their obligations to scholarship and their students'. There is, therefore, no case for the changes embodied in the Bill. 'These will place higher education for the first time directly under state control in a manner which will threaten its character, its freedom and its quality.' Change is needed, but proposals 'should be properly considered in a separate Bill', not slipped through Parliament 'as a postscript to the government's massive and controversial legislation on our schools'.

This chapter has considered government policy in two disparate, but extremely important, areas – the ILEA and further and higher education. This completes the analysis of structural changes embodied in the Bill. We may now turn to the other main area of concern – that related to the whole field of curriculum and assessment (including testing) in the schools, which forms, in fact, the first 'Chapter' (or set of clauses) in the Education 'Reform' Bill.

### Notes and References

1 Greenwich, Lewisham, Tower Hamlets, Hackney, Islington, Southwark, Lambeth, Camden, City of Westminster, Kensington and Chelsea, Wandsworth, Hammersmith and Fulham, and the City of London.

2 Obtainable from the National Union of Teachers, Hamilton House, Mabledon Place, London WC1.

# 4 The Curriculum and Testing

## 1 The Proposals

The Education Bill, as is well known, includes a set of clauses (1 to 16) embodying in legislative form detailed provisions both for 'A National Curriculum' for all pupils in maintained schools between the ages of five and sixteen, and for administering to these pupils sets (or 'batteries') of tests covering all subjects in the curriculum at the ages of seven, eleven, fourteen and sixteen. According to Kenneth Baker, this is an 'historic' reform.

It might seem that the Secretary of State is on firmer ground, in terms of the time allowed for 'consultation' when he argues that there has been much discussion of the curriculum over the last ten years or so. What he does not mention, however, is that much of it has been severely critical of the increasingly energetic and even ruthless thrust towards central control in this area, both from local authorities and teachers. A MORI poll taken in the summer showed that 65 per cent of teachers believe that the Secretary of State has sought too much power in running schools (*TES*, 12 June 1987). It is, however, fair to say that there probably is a broad consensus that a common core of subjects (or activities) is desirable – even a common curriculum. Those who pioneered the move to comprehensive education back in the 1950s and early 1960s (this author included) certainly believed that here was an opportunity to offer *all* pupils access to knowledge, science and culture, and that to differentiate the curriculum for different groups of children is arbitrary, unjust and divisive, indeed negates the main objective of comprehensive education.

But those so arguing, then and now, hold that, if generally accepted 'guidelines' covering the curriculum were to be offered, these must be *guidelines* and not precisely defined 'programmes of study', and further, that these should be determined as a result of full and democratic discussion by all those involved, particularly teachers. They also argue that a forum be established for discussion of such matters where plans and proposals can be evolved. The idea that the government – any government – should lay down in *legislative* form a precisely defined curriculum, covering all the main subjects for children of all ages between five (possibly four) and sixteen; and that the content and balance of this curriculum should be determined by the Secretary of State (advised presumably by civil servants who are not educationists, and have not themselves had any experience of actually teaching children) is and always has been entirely unacceptable. The result is likely to be a massive alienation of teachers who, if this proposal is actually implemented, will find themselves increasingly deskilled and downgraded. Harry Judge, formerly a comprehensive head and now Director of the Department of Educational Studies at Oxford University, put the issue clearly when the consultation paper first appeared. Teachers, he said, would be 'shackled' to a national curriculum in the worst traditions of centralised countries; Baker's leglisation would turn teachers into 'an oppressed bureaucracy' (*TES*, 17 July 1987).

The main proposals in the original consultative document, some of which had more publicity than others, can be briefly summarised. There is to be a 'National Curriculum' for all, consisting of eight 'foundation' subjects (or subject areas). Three of these – English, mathematics and 'combined sciences' – are allotted a special status as 'Core' subjects to which 30 to 40 per cent of the time should be given. The other five recognised compulsory subjects are defined as technology, a modern foreign language, history/geography or history *or* geography, art/music/drama/design (one subject area, presumably), and physical education. All pupils (apparently from the age of *five*) must study *all* 'foundation' subjects. An example of the time breakdown is given only for years four and five at the secondary stage. Here, it was originally proposed, between 75 and 85 per cent of teaching time should be devoted to the foundation subjects. The remaining time (oddly presented in the paper as comprising 10 per cent of the total time) can be devoted to 'additional subjects' (those listed total eleven). But religious education, already required by statute (under the 1944 Act), figured in the original paper simply as one of the eleven 'additional subjects' which 'might be taken for GCSE'. If this is regarded as compulsory the time available for others is reduced to below 10 per cent. If we assume the typical 'traditional' grammar school type timetable, which DES officials, probably having experienced it themselves, clearly had in mind – seven periods a day for five days a week – this left precisely three-and-a-half periods of 40 minutes each week for those 'additional' subjects listed as perhaps appropriate for the fifteen to sixteen year old age group. Into that time must also be fitted first, religious education, defined by Baker late in November as 'a compulsory additional subject' which must be taught for 'a reasonable time' each week, as well as such popular subjects as home economics, a second foreign language, business studies, information technology, careers guidance, personal and social development (a growing area), not to mention peace studies (unpopular with this government). Not that all these appear on the official list of possible 'additional' subjects, which itself is narrow and unimaginative.

As a result of a unanimous outcry against this nonsense, Baker, at the last minute (the end of November), announced certain concessions. The foundation subjects, he said, need not take up 90 per cent (or whatever) of the school timetable. No precise percentage would be laid down. It would be 'up to the schools ... to "deliver"' the national curriculum, etc., etc. In other words, final decisions would lie in the hands of the Secretary of State who might, benevolently, run things a little more loosely than appeared from the consultation paper. On the other hand, of course, he or she might do the opposite (no time schedules are laid down in the relevant clause of the Bill; all this sort of 'detail' will be left to later 'orders' issued – perhaps after 'consultation' by the Secretary of State). But at least a *verbal* concession has been made, for what that's worth.

The original consultation paper envisaged that very precise and detailed 'programmes of study' for each subject would be drawn up and given full legislative authority – presumably deviation will constitute an offence. These programmes are to be recommended to the Secretary of State by 'Working Groups' consisting of individuals he or she appoints.

These will 'set out the overall content, knowledge, skills and processes' which children 'should be taught ...', specifying 'in more detail' a minimum of common content. All this is spelt out more fully in letters addressed by Baker to the already appointed science and mathematics working groups, which have been at work since July. In these the Secretary of State lays down that reports are expected to embody '*a detailed description*' of the content, skills and processes all pupils 'need to be taught'. Further, 'attainment' targets (needed for testing) must be defined, and Baker stresses 'the importance of specificity' in their definition. In effect, he required these working groups, consisting of teachers and others, to produce within *three months* (by 30 November) 'interim' reports covering the central features of an eleven-year programme, together with very specifically defined attainment targets – throughout the age range, presumably – with extreme rapidity. Press reports indicate that the maths working group, from which so much was expected (basically the legitimisation of the whole procedures) has been unable to reach agreement, and that its report 'will be a grave set-back for the Secretary of State'. Members have complained of lack of time, and of too much 'direction' from Her Majesty's Inspectors. More important, perhaps, has been the inability of the group members to agree as to whether there should be national arrangements for testing and assessment at all! (*Independent*, 30 November 1987)[1] The date set for the final reports of these two groups (maths and science) is 30 June 1988. The intention is to set up a further series of groups covering all the main 'foundation' subjects.

One of the most controversial proposals in the entire Bill, as is well known, is that concerning legislative imposition of mass testing for all pupils in maintained schools at the ages of seven ('or thereabouts') eleven, fourteen and sixteen. It is for this purpose that the Curriculum Working Groups must define precise 'attainment targets'. 'At the heart of the assessment process' states the official document 'will be nationally prescribed tests' to be 'done' by 'all pupils'. These will be administered and monitored by teachers but 'externally moderated'. To prepare for this an 'expert' body, a 'Task Group on Assessment and Testing' was appointed last August, by the Secretary of State, of course. Its remit was 'to make recommendations on the common elements of an assessment strategy' for *all* subjects and to report within four months – 'by Christmas'! A deep confusion about this whole topic is apparent in a crucial paragraph in the Secretary of State's instruction to this group. Are the same tests to be taken by *all* children (as Thatcher appears to want) or has the Task Group been asked to prepare different tests targeted at different levels of so-called 'ability' at each age?[2] The matter was further complicated when, on 2 November, nearly three months after the Task Group began work – and only a few weeks before its report was due – Baker despatched a further letter of 'guidance'. This now defined three purposes for the exercise. But this merely made confusion worse confounded, as will shortly appear.

Mass testing is given a central role in the document, as it has in government policy. Whatever has since been said, there can be not the slightest doubt that, in the government's eyes, the bulk of testing must be conducted with what are known (in the trade) as 'norm-referenced tests', the only type that can claim a modicum of 'objectivity' or base in scientific procedures. But this, of course, is precisely the form of test formerly used in the old, discredited, 11-plus examination (in 'intelligence', mathematics, English). Such tests arrange children in a hierarchy (equivalent to what statisticians call a 'normal distribution curve'). This is a statistical concept, but what this means in practice is that all such tests are designed to produce a pattern of results which show a few children at the top end with high marks, a roughly equivalent number at the bottom gaining few marks, the bulk of the rest distributed between the two extremes, largely bunched at and around the average mark (or mean).

The reason why this must be the type of test the government intends to use can be deduced from the stress the consultation paper lays on the need for *comparative* assessments between individual children, between different classes in the same school, between other schools in the LEA 'or neighbourhood' between LEAs generally and nationally. In short, what is planned is a massive series of competitions, at all levels, based on test results. Nor is this all; great emphasis is also put on the need for publicity. Test results must be made available to individual pupils and parents, to teachers, to parents generally and governing bodies; also to employers and the local community, to LEAs, and finally at national level, to *'central government, Parliament and the public'* (emphasis in the original). Statistical data of the kind required for such a publicity exercise can only be provided by the old type of 'norm referenced' tests. Tests designed specifically to probe a pupil's weaknesses (and strengths) with the objective of clarifying remedial treatment could not conceivably answer – these are 'diagnostic tests' discussed below.

What is the government's timetable for all this?

The first set of 'Orders' relating to attainment targets and study programmes for maths and science should be made early in 1989, to be implemented in the schools at the start of the academic year 1989-90. Tests should begin at once. Similar steps for other subjects would follow so the whole procedures are in operation from the summer of 1991. This, says the document, 'is a challenging timetable'.

A number of other points made may be briefly referred to. Pupils having a statement of 'special need' (under the 1981 Education Act) should have specified in their statement a note of any aspect of the national curriculum requirements that should not apply. But curriculum requirements may apply to four-year old children in classes mainly for those aged five and over. A 'National Curriculum Council' is to be established (one for England, another for Wales), in place of the existing, non-statutory, School Curriculum Development Council (clause 7). This will consist of individuals appointed personally by the Secretary of State; no elected representatives of any professional or other interested organisation will have membership; the Council is to be restricted to an advisory capacity. The Secretary of State will also exercise his or her personal choice to fill a 'School Examination and Assessment Council' to advise on this aspect (also clause 7). Reports on 'the implementation of the national curriculum' will be required from HMIs (Her Majesty's Inspectors), although there is also a suggestion that LEA advisers may be hijacked into assisting in monitoring its 'delivery'. A full page of the document is devoted to explaining how complaints about 'delivery of the national curriculum' are to be dealt with. More significant is the admission that the government intends to implement the whole process described (including a massive testing programme) 'within the planned level of resources', i.e. with no extra cash.[3]

Finally it need cause no surprise that the 'National' Curriculum, and all the rest (testing, etc.), is to apply only to publicly maintained schools. All independent (including 'public') schools are to be exempt, as well as the government's cherished city technology colleges.

## 2    The Critique: Curriculum

'DES Postbag Fills With Disquiet' headlined the *Times Educational Supplement* (9 October 1987) at the close of the few weeks allowed for discussion. After a period of generalised, if very lively, debate little seemed to have been sorted out. No less than 5,000 written responses had arrived at the DES in the final week. But these 'do not seem to add much to what has already been said'.

But who could have scanned them to come up with so quick a summary? Responses ranged from the detailed analysis and critique, running to over 7,000 words, from the Sheffield Education Committee, and the very thorough and sharp criticism from leading specialists in the field of Special Education, to short, punchy comments from a very wide variety of public bodies, educational organisations and individuals. The totally farcical nature of the 'consultation' appears most ridiculous – or, better, most cynical – in the case of this specific document packed with highly controversial assertions about the curriculum, including imposition of mass testing techniques which many believe could herald the death of education in any true sense.

'The National Curriculum and its associated testing' is intended 'to focus public discontent on individual schools and teachers', warned the *Times Educational Supplement* when the document first appeared (31 July 1987). The whole burden of the 'reform', is an 'expression of distrust of teachers', and a belief that 'just about every educated person ... knows what teachers should be doing better than the teachers'. That is one view. Another is that the whole exercise is basically about social control – testing and grading from the age of seven ('or thereabouts') will ensure that everyone 'knows their place' (in the words of the DES official quoted earlier) while total control of the content of education in all the main 'foundation' subjects will minimise the threat of dangerous thoughts creeping into schools. This is why some responses, that of the independent educational journal *Forum* is an example, assess the move to 'draconian legislation' to control the curriculum as 'appropriate to a totalitarian regime'. No evidence is advanced that could in any way justify so dramatic a move.

The main criticisms to hand on the curriculum proposals may now be summarised, although without assigning these between organisations as before since the tendency is towards unanimity.

*Dirigiste* procedures are a major concern. Legislation authorising the Secretary of State to appoint a National Curriculum Council to advise on the entire content of teaching is widely regarded as an unacceptable departure from appropriate democractic practice. At the very least, such a body should comprise representatives chosen by organisations of the teaching profession, local authorities and parents, along with particular interested parties such as the churches and ethnic minorities. Such a body could act both as a forum for discussion and advice to the Secretary of State, not simply as a cog in the transmission machinery he or she manipulates.

Another main concern is with the prevailing academicism of the proposed curriculum. This is defined entirely in terms of 'subjects', as was the case when the central authority last intervened in this area 80 years ago. '1904 and All That', the *Times Educational Supplement* (31 July 1987) aptly headed its main leader on the topic. It was then the aim 'to ensure that new secondary schools adopted the traditional grammar school model'. In 1987, in a rapidly changing context, the government reiterates this discredited model, modified only by the inclusion of 'technology' as a foundation subject. This certainly makes glaringly obvious the kind of thinking likely to emanate from an ossified bureaucracy at the centre – or was it Baker himself who thought this one up? Thinking of this order – if such it can be called – ignores recent developments in primary and secondary schools; the development of new curricula and procedures matching modern developments in knowledge and in educational practice and *all* the major contributions to curriculum theory and practice. There have been the Hargreaves Report (*Improving Secondary Schools*) for the ILEA in 1983, the proposals of such broadly based bodies as the 'Education for Capability' movement, or 'Education 2000'. In no sense whatever can the proposals, defined in terms of three core and other arbitrarily chosen 'foundation' subjects, apparently excluding all other areas until the fourth year in secondary school, be seen as a forward looking solution to the inherent problems with which schools have been struggling in their endeavours to equip adolescents to understand

and cope with the complexities of the society in which they are growing up. In sum, the curriculum document appears to most commentators as a typical product of a remote, managerially inclined bureaucracy without any understanding of the term 'education'. The basic, frequently reiterated, assumption is that a curriculum is something teachers 'deliver' to children – as if it were a package of fish and chips. But education concerns the development of human abilities and skills, and thereby the acquisition and 'mastery' of knowledge – not merely 'absorption' of selected facts. Small wonder, then, that the term 'motivation', which so concerns the dedicated teacher, is absent from the official dicta to which Kenneth Baker has so proudly put his name.

English primary schools have been the envy of the world, and have certainly developed new approaches to teaching, generally recognised as highly effective. Those concerned to build on these developments are deeply worried about the clear attempt to force subject-based teaching back into the primary school, to the exclusion of an integrated approach based on inquiry which has so manifestly improved the learning process. Separately identified subject programmes, it is argued, are likely to emanate from the discrete subject working groups, each of which is to operate independently, and at breakneck speed, to meet Kenneth Baker's deadlines. These programmes, to be enforced by regulations, are likely to destroy the evolving unified curriculum, and return primary schools to the fragmented, subject-focussed curriculum of the distant past.

Multicultural approaches and practices have been a feature of recent developments, in tune with the needs of a multicultural society, but official proposals are carefully framed to make no mention of these, though they reflect the recommendations of the Swann Report and have met with a high degree of success and even moderate government support. Clearly space is needed in the curriculum under this heading, but no allowance is made. And this recalls the recent statement by Baroness Hooper (the government's education minister in the House of Lords), that separate schools for ethnic minorities may come if parents demand these – a clear intimation that government proposals hang together on this issue as on others, even to the level of promoting 'apartheid' in the school system.

More generally, the imposition of a national curriculum from above is seen as a serious blow to initiative whether on the part of teachers or local authorities where much has been done to promote curriculum *development*. Inevitably it would lead to constriction of work which has taken place in particular schools, groups of schools, local authority areas. Sheffield is engaged in a highly imaginative and successful curriculum reform project covering all schools in the area, both primary and secondary, with the aim of evolving new subject groupings and teaching plans in line with the rapid developments in science and technology, including those relating to teaching practice. All such creative work – bringing together teachers, local authority advisers, university and polytechnic teachers and researchers – will be undermined or eliminated if the government's plans are permitted to materialise. Much more, which has been going on quietly at school level, in so far as the heavy cuts in equipment and resources imposed by the government have allowed, will also be laid waste. Indeed, everything that enlightened teachers have been working for most of their lives, as Harry Rée, a distinguished school head and university professor during his career and still teaching in comprehensive schools in retirement, protested as soon as plans materialised (*Independent*, 29 July 1987).

A particular cause for disquiet is the lack of attention to the 'special educational needs' of pupils who suffer from learning difficulties, or handicaps, of one kind or another – sometimes a combination of several. Specialists in this area warn that the proposals tabled for these pupils may result 'in the very state that they are designed to remedy'. About 20 per cent of the school population come within this category. New procedures for assessing and meeting their needs were introduced following the recommendations of the Warnock Report embodied in the Education Act of 1981. The only reference the Secretary of State and his officials make to these needs, typically enough, is the bureacratic comment that 'statements' about incapacity must detail the bits of the standard curriculum from which they may be excused. In short, say those concerned with special education, the consultation document 'takes no account of the major purposes or provisions' of the 1981 Act. Its 'internal inconsistencies' in commenting on individual differences and the manner in which the policy advanced might be implemented 'make it difficult to see how intended aims are to be achieved without detriment to the quality of education'. As confused is the thinking about curriculum for children with learning difficulties. This must be varied to meet individual needs but that cannot be when specific age-related targets are set and these are likely to mean the labelling as failures of handicapped children whose test results fall below average achievement.

That experts in this field are acutely unhappy comes clearly across in the memorandum cited which has more to say about mass testing.[4] The same impression emerges from several articles in the relevant specialist journals.[5]

The philistinism of these official plans for the curriculum emerges most clearly, perhaps, from protests about subjects excluded from attention or considered only as additions which must fight for a place. Predictably, there has been sustained outcry from supporters of classical subjects, notably Latin, which is taught on a small scale in some ILEA comprehensive schools and elsewhere and should undoubtedly continue without interference. At the other end of the scale is home economics, which achieves mention only as an 'additional subject' and so must joust with many others for a share in the non-prescribed teaching time. According to the latest survey 34 per cent of pupils take this in years four and five in secondary schools but 76 per cent in years one and two from which, on current plans, it would be totally excluded! Careers education is another widely developed and extremely 'relevant' subject entered on by 66 per cent of the fourth year and 64 per cent of the fifth. It does not receive so much as a nod, let alone an intelligent mention, in the Baker proposals, but is *totally excluded*. The same goes for the varied teaching of adolescents, school leavers and potential job seekers under the heading 'personal and social education' – an area now encompassing some 54 per cent of fourth and fifth year boys and girls. All this information is, of course, at the disposal of the DES which has just published figures relating to 1984, the latest information drawn on here. It is also apparent that fourth and fifth year pupils would spend *less time* on mathematics and English under the new dispensation than they currently do.[6] This seems the opposite of the expressed intention.

The plight of religious education has already been mentioned. It does not figure as a 'foundation' subject, but as an 'additional' subject. However under the 1944 Act, which still holds, it is already a compulsory subject – the only one to which this applies, and, as already mentioned, it is now defined as 'a compulsory additional subject'. Allot to it one period a week and, even after the Baker concession mentioned earlier, there remains little time for all other 'excluded' and 'additional' subjects. Well, Ministers try to extricate themselves, so now such subjects can 'enter into' foundation subjects. Not so, when the latter have a programme precisely defined by specialists. To unravel the curriculum proposals involves a descent into absurdity, the outcome (as the *Financial Times* has suggested) of too little thought, or care, by bureaucrats unashamed to issue what looks like a tidy scheme but turns out to be full of holes.

## 3   The Critique of Testing

The most profound hostility – demonstratively expressed on at least two occasions – has been registered towards mass testing of all children from about seven, and at eleven, fourteen and sixteen. There is, of course, experience of what this means especially among teachers. Even those too young to have had personal experience have heard what was the effect of the procedures involved, for this has entered deeply into the folklore of every school. Parents have also learned what 'the 11-plus' meant. No one wants a repitition of this experience which

was so profoundly harmful to children and their
education – as the government well understands.
Hence attempts to cover up its intention to introduce
anew the same old discredited type of test, moves
which only serve to underline the frightening
ignorance of present education Ministers and
apparently also their advisers. Teachers do not need
to be told what it is all about and have underlined
that every opposition will be mounted to the threat.
'Details of the assessment and tests at seven, eleven
and fourteen still have to be worked out,' wrote the
*Times Educational Supplement* (31 July 1987) on
the original issue of the consultative document.
'Nothing diminishes the impression that they are
certain to exercise a malign influence on teaching in
many schools.'

Two Ministers have had the temerity to tangle
publicly with teachers and educationists on this
issue – not the more experienced Kenneth Baker
who has astutely kept away from serious *public*
discussion of his proposals, but his subordinates.
First the accident prone Angela Rumbold, at a
conference on primary education organised by the
National Association of Head Teachers in October,
succeeded in 'galvanising her audience' to rally to
'the call of … their President, for non-co-operation',
should Mr Baker continue to 'insist on no
concessions'. Ready to pre-empt the report of the
special 'Task Force', still formulating advice on this
issue, she made her own contribution to defending
the declared intention of publishing league table
comparisons of test results from different schools. 'I
do not believe that parents will make naïve
judgments on the basis of league tables,' the
Minister went on – according to a full report of this
meeting – 'to hoots of derision from her audience of

150 primary heads', talked down to beyond
endurance by one who clearly did not know what she
was talking about, and who had earlier patronised
not only the professionalism of teachers but also the
level of understanding of parents. Classwork in
some primary schools, Angela Rumbold informed
the teachers, 'consists of amorphous discussion and
idle play'! The 'national curriculum' is defined in
subject terms for parents who 'need to have things
described to them in simple, clear language' – a
dictum met with cries of 'shame'. As for the
government, it must have 'proof' of rising standards
in the form of 'regular national tests'. By the time
question time arrived 'the audience had grown
openly critical and angry' as experienced teachers
sought to educate the Minister, explaining the
'direct contradiction between tests used for diagnostic purposes' and the kind of test results 'from
which league tables could be consulted'. Some of this
appeared on television for the instruction of the
public before the Minister managed to escape.

'Bad Times for Mrs Rumbold', commented an
editorial accompanying this report (*TES*, 16 October
1987). 'Her gloss on the national curriculum
consultation paper certainly helped to raise the
temperature of a group of professionals among
whom the government might have expected to
number many friends' – given no earlier tendency
among primary heads to break up meetings by
discomfiting Ministers. 'A disastrous combination of
patronising condescension and palpable ignorance
antagonised most of her audience.' Many of her
listeners 'found it difficult to believe that anyone
who had actually held down the job of an education
committee chairman in an outer London borough,
and in the Association of Metropolitan Authorities,

could show such a crass lack of sensitivity to the
concerns of a professional audience'. It seems the
Tory educational 'revolution' (as Baker puts it) is
spearheaded by ignorance leaning on an equally
remote bureaucracy.

The second confrontation, less traumatic perhaps,
involved the other junior education Minister
propping up the Baker plans, Bob Dunn (he of the
Solihull adventure, mentioned above). He faced a
250-strong gathering of educationists at Warwick
University in late October where he first sparked off
derision by admitting that 'open enrolment', as
insisted upon by Baker and Thatcher, 'would cause
"some" problems for LEAs'. They all laughed again,
reported the *TES* (23 October 1987) when he
followed this up by saying that the proposed tests
'would not tell parents "everything" about their
children'. The Minister shortly retired from the
platform, to another chorus of 'shame', refusing to
stay for questions on the excuse of a busy timetable.
Some resemblance here to jesting Pilate, perhaps,
who would not stay for an answer. There has been
little in the way of common sense, let alone truth, in
ministerial pronouncements.

Once more, at the annual conference of the
Campaign for the Advancement of State Education –
a knowledgeable organisation composed largely of
parents – overwhelming opposition was expressed to
the very principle of comparative testing. 'Poisonous'
has been the adjective applied to the Baker Bill by
Joan Sallis, a leading figure in CASE. The
conference passed unanimously a call that the
testing proposals be dropped. 'I'm not prepared to
have my child's future laid on the line based on one
day's testing,' declared the vice-chair of Bath CASE
claiming support for the views expressed from

parents' leaders in Avon, who would also deliberately withdraw children. In sum, CASE seemed on the way to countering official determination to indulge in benchmark assessment by a demand that parents be accorded the right to opt out of this. An aspect of which the government is bound to take account, suggested the *TES*, summing up this report, if it is serious about honouring parental rights (25 September 1987; see also Barbara McLaughlin's letter, 9 October 1987). Trouble ahead?

'There is a resounding chorus against tests that identify failures from age seven onwards, and that exist in order to create league tables in which schools move up and down,' commented the *Independent* on 7 October. 'The message from the responses to the consultative document is overwhelming: it registers acceptance, even approval, of diagnostic testing, the kind which teases out children who are falling behind and need extra help,' as against the deepest hostility towards the kind of tests needed to provide league tables, as advocated by the government.

There is not the slightest doubt of the government's intention in respect of tests, just as there is little doubt that its overriding aims are populist and political with no inclination towards educational considerations. 'Parents, governing bodies, employers, and the local community', the official document underlines, 'should know what a school's assessment and examination results indicate about performance *and how they compare* with those of other schools within the LEA or neighbourhood.' All 'interested parties' must have 'appropriate and readily digestible information' as to 'what is being taught and achieved'. Not the slightest interest is shown, in the consultation papers, in diagnostic testing. Indeed it seems the civil servants who drew up the document knew nothing about the complications, or the various purposes of testing, or of the different types of test required. Public response to the document, particularly from teachers, has been such that Baker has been forced (despite protestations that he is immoveable) to move somewhat – but only to confound the confusion yet further.

There is a world of difference between tests designed to produce data for league tables, and serious diagnostic analysis. The former are mass pencil-and-paper games (anything else would be far too expensive) susceptible to rapid machine marking which assigns a single figure on each test for each child. This makes it easy to tot up averages for classes or schools which may then be compared.

The diagnostic test is totally different. The object is to diagnose the specific learning problems an individual child may have; or a particular learning difficulty preventing the mastery of key concepts in a specific area, for instance, mathematics. The intention is to discover, by such probing, precisely where a child's weakness lies. The teacher may then assist the child to overcome the problem so that learning accompanies teaching and the way is prepared for moving on to the next stage. This kind of 'test' does not produce a result expressed as a figure, nor would there be the slightest point in attaching one to what is a continuing educational *process*.

Fundamental differences from the paper-and-pencil test may be summarised under two heads. First, the diagnostic test requires *very* detailed information about the individual child – over a *wide range* of activity, possibly close observation of this by the tester or teacher. Second, the test is of no value unless it aims to expose both strengths *and weaknesses* – the latter are always important to an educationist. Clearly the idea of ranging schools on 'league tables' according to test results is not one to encourage exposure of weaknesses; on the contrary, as high a result as possible for each individual pupil would be the aim. And this, as is so well known as not to require repetition, forces teachers to *teach to the test*, however over-simplified and narrowed down the subject is. The traditional example in the history of education is the era of 'payment by results' when teachers' pay depended directly on their aptitude in training pupils to hoodwink inspectors who, in those days, conducted the examinations personally.

No one working in this field, with any knowledge of the situation, holds that the same tests can be used *both* for diagnostic purposes *and* for comparative (league table) purposes. The Assessment of Performance Unit, which engages in 'light sampling' across the main subjects, uses tests designed essentially to obtain a statistical outcome allowing comparisons – as between gender or ethnic differences, for instance. It has moved the technology of testing forward to some degree, especially in the area of science, but is not in any sense involved in diagnostic testing.

The views put here are those held unanimously by all the leading researchers in the area of testing and assessment. Two of these, Harvey Goldstein and Margaret Brown (Professor of Statistical Measurement and Reader in Mathematical Education at London University respectively) state very clearly the falsity of the claim that the same test may be used 'for both diagnostic and monitoring functions' (letter to the *Guardian*, 27 October 1987).

To their knowledge, they write, 'nobody has yet demonstrated that these two functions can be properly combined in a simple assessment; any which purport to do so could be highly misleading'. A specific challenge was then issued to the National Federation of Educational Research (NFER) on this precise issue, since this claim had apparently been made by that body. In response the director, Clare Burstall, corroborated the view that the two functions could not be combined in a single test. 'Some tests are offered for monitoring and other tests are offered for diagnosis', she wrote, of the NFER tests. Referring to a section in that body's response entitled 'Different Tests for Different Purposes', she added 'two types of test would be required to provide the information specified in the consultation paper' (letter to the *Guardian*, 3 November 1987). 'The government should look very carefully at ... claims' that the two functions can be served by one test, Goldstein and Brown concluded, 'before it institutes any national system of testing'.

This is an appropriate point to introduce a response by the national body representing virtually all educational researchers working in universities, polytechnics and other bodies concerned. 'We write', runs a personal letter to Kenneth Baker, 'from the largest annual gathering of educational researchers in Britain – the British Educational Research Association' (BERA). Attention should be paid to research which, 'through its attention to the canons of systematic enquiry, sustained analysis and public scrutiny' has an important contribution to make. Proposals in the Education Bill, however, 'fly in the face of accumulated evidence'. If adopted 'they will divide, disrupt and demoralise' the education service 'to a degree unparalleled in the history of state-maintained schooling'. In particular, continued the letter from BERA (which includes many experts on assessment), 'The introduction of benchmark testing looks set to restage the human tragedies that surrounded the nineteenth century practice of "payment by results" and the post-1944 implementation of 11-plus selection.' (*Research Intelligence* (BERA), October 1987)

Added to protests from researchers, parents, teachers, were others from those involved in teaching and examining. The General Certificate of Secondary Education (GCSE) examination boards, which will have the function of 'moderating' such testing (and the prospect of gaining millions of new 'customers') have expressed 'grave doubts' about the possibility of meeting the objectives set by the government. In this case it is experts in the matter of examining, assessing and moderating who are reported as 'far from convinced it will be possible to produce reliable and valid means of carrying out assessment and testing of younger pupils' in the way that seems intended by the government. 'We need to be sure what the purposes of the tests are,' a representative of the boards told the *Times Educational Supplement* (10 September 1987). 'We have had nothing but conflicting information from Ministers who, on the one hand, say they are diagnostic and, on the other, claim they are to measure attainment.' 'They cannot have both,' he concluded. Before there can be any 'pressing ahead with legislation' objectives require to be clarified and the feasibility of proposed procedures assessed. An almost unprecedented rap over the knuckles from those who will be loaded with the full responsibility for carrying the proposals through in practice.

Teachers of mathematics, of science and of

English belong to special associations whose deep concern has also been expressed – and these, after all, are the people to be involved in teaching key, or core, subjects of the 'national curriculum'.[7] All have joined together in unanimously expressing 'serious misgivings' about the testing proposals. These 'could depress', rather than raise, 'standards in schools', especially among 'average and low-achieving pupils confronted with failure'. The likelihood would be that 'testing could dominate and constrain the curriculum', leading to 'teaching to the test'. As for early testing, to be valid this 'has to involve close and time-consuming observation of single pupils and small groups carrying out a range of practical tasks' (*TES*, 2 October 1987). This is the *professionals'* view.

By contrast Baker's document, launched in triumphalist terms, claimed testing as 'a proven and essential way towards raising standards of achievement'. Where is the evidence to support this claim, asks a leading expert on the issue, Roger Murphy, Director of the Assessment and Examinations Unit at Southampton University? Declaring himself in favour of 'an appropriate and vigorous system of pupil assessment', Murphy describes the age-related testing required by Baker as 'ill conceived and misguided'. Current proposals are 'potentially disruptive and likely to do enormous damage to the quality' of maintained schools. It is now recognised throughout the world that large scale testing schemes are 'major barriers to the raising of educational standards'. They have led teachers 'to teach pupils to pass tests' at the expense of 'developing the full range of pupil strength and offering remedial help for weaknesses'. In sum the consultation paper draws largely on 'ideas behind the old 11-plus examination', taking no account of new, positive developments such as moves towards Records of Achievement. To look back to that period, Murphy concludes choosing the appropriate term deliberately, 'is crazy' (*TES*, 16 October 1987).

It may have been the continuous build up of informed but universally critical responses that prompted the Secretary of State, at the end of October, to direct new instructions to his portentously named 'Task Group on Assessment and Testing', redefining their job. This long suffering group of assessment experts had been at work since August with a remit to outline recommendations by Christmas – or offer advice which (it may be supposed) must at all costs seek respectability. Now the orders were abruptly changed, half-way through the four-month period allotted, in a letter so lengthy, tortuous and involved that it defies summary. There could hardly be a stronger hint that Baker was experiencing doubts as to how to maintain the impetus of this 'great reform', for the letter has a flavour of arrogant bullying coupled with pleas for advice. The Task Group is required to advance practicable recommendations to be implemented in a cost-effective way. But the Secretary of State also requires 'advice on a coherent national system for assessment and testing in relation to agreed attainment targets' which also 'recognises the different purposes to which assessment is put' and 'how they interrelate with and complement each other' while 'bearing in mind the points I set out in paragraph 5 above' ... etc., etc.

It would seem that the crucial difference between diagnostic and monitoring testing is accepted – though it might also seem that the group is asked to cover both aspects – and more! An amazingly confused paragraph, lengthy and self-contradictory, follows, relating to whether or not tests (and curricula, or 'targets', which are not in the Task Group's brief) are to be differentiated by 'ability'. But the trend of the letter is clear enough, despite the convoluted verbiage, what is most stressed is that *'nationally prescribed tests'* are needed and the Task Group is required to come up with advice convenient to the government. It will be interesting to assess the outcome but the interim report, if it is produced by Christmas 1987 as instructed, will be too late for comment here, although it has proved possible to include a brief mention in the postscript.

It was underlined at the outset of this book that the government's policy relating to the school system is all of a piece, that it hangs together. The kernel of the concern has now been investigated – the plans to enforce a given curriculum closely linked to 'benchmark' testing. But it is this very aspect that is most firmly condemned by specialists, complementing protests by teachers, parents and LEAs. There has been more than one appeal to history, not merely the 11-plus debacle but the disastrous situation created in late Victorian England 'when the vast majority of children were educated only to pass exams,' in the words of Denis Lawton, Director of the University of London Institute of Education, and Clyde Chitty in *Forum* (Autumn 1987). The proposal for a national curriculum must be freed 'from the accompanying notion of age-related benchmark testing' which could only operate 'as a straitjacket' on the entire system. Above all, they conclude, we need to convince the government that their plans 'will acquire no credibility with educationists and teachers' while a national curriculum continues to be viewed by politicians and civil servants as 'a bureaucratic device for exercising control over what goes on in schools'. Yet this appears the main objective of the whole exercise to the two authors of this recent article. There are many who will agree.

And perhaps, in conclusion, it is worth pointing out that the few early clauses of the Bill relating to all this are framed in such a way as to devolve a waterproof totality of powers on the Secretary of State personally: powers to determine every aspect of the curriculum between the ages of five and sixteen, and every aspect of its testing and assessment. The exercise of these total(itarian) powers are subject only to 'advice' from the two new bodies (for curriculum and for examinations) consisting entirely (that is, without exception) of the Secretary of State's nominees, on topics 'as he may refer' to them, or as they 'may see fit'. The latter phrase contains the single loophole for criticism, or alternative suggestions.

The Secretary of State will exercise these powers by making 'orders', e.g. concerning, let's say, a specific programme of study, which is sent to the National Curriculum Council for report. 'Consultations' are then to take place before the said body submits its report, which will be published. The Secretary of State may then publish a draft of the proposed order; allow one month for consultation, etc., after which 'the Secretary of State may make the order, with or without modifications' (clause 11).

In the light of the very evident and almost total contempt this government (and especially Mr Baker) has shown for the process of 'consultation' required for this Bill, these procedures, recently claimed by Baker as proof that he is *not* arrogating dictatorial powers, carry no conviction whatever.

The full intention to assume total centralised control over the entire curriculum is absolutely apparent, and it is as well that *everyone* should be very clear about this.[8]

## Notes and References

1 In the past three months, reported John Fairhall in the *Guardian* (18 November 1987), 'the group has not got beyond setting out the general issues and problems'. Several of its thirteen members 'are prepared to resign if Mr Baker hardens his proposals'. Another comment states that the group's members 'are not prepared to pretend that they can deliver what [Mr Baker] wanted in the time allowed ... and retain their integrity'. (*TES*, 4 December 1987)

2 The paragraph, headed 'Differentiation' reads as follows:
I am looking to you to recommend attainment targets which set out the knowledge, skills and understanding which pupils *of different abilities* should be able to achieve by the end of the school year in which they reach one of the key ages. They should allow scope for the very able, those of average ability, and the less able to show what they can do. So far as possible *I want to avoid having different attainment targets for children of different levels of ability*. I shall expect you to justify any essential exceptions from this principle. In general I seek targets for each of the key ages *which may be attempted and assessed at a range of levels*, and which challenge each child to do the best that he or she can. (My emphasis, B.S.)

3 Although, under 'Financial Effects of the Bill', the Bill itself states that additional expenditure will be incurred 'rising to £33 million in 1990-91'. This covers the costs of the two councils (for curriculum and examinations), and 'an element for research and development particularly in the areas of assessment and testing, and the administration of the assessment arrangements'. It looks as if most of this is to go on test development and its administration.

4 The memorandum is signed by sixteen leading specialists in the field of children with special educational needs. These include Professors Klaus Wedell (London University), Peter Mittler (Manchester University), Robert Gulliford (Birmingham University) and two former HMIs in this area, John Fish and John Garrett.

5 For instance, Will Swann, 'The Educational Consequence of Mr Baker', *Special Children*, September 1987; Wilf Brennan, 'Once More into the Core', *Special Children*, October 1987.

6 *TES*, 6 November 1987. The data on 1984 patterns are derived from *The 1984 Secondary School Staffing Survey: data on the curriculum in maintained secondary schools in England*, DES *Statistical Bulletin*, 10/87.

7 These are, National Association for the Teaching of English, Association for Science Education, Association of Teachers of Mathematics – all long-standing and prestigious associations of professionals deeply concerned with their subject.

8 Even the smallest deviation from the 'National Curriculum' for developmental purposes is to be closely monitored and carried on only under the most stringent conditions. Clause 9 lays it down that, to enable 'development work or experiments to be carried out', the Secretary of State 'may direct as respects a particular maintained school that, for such a period as may be specified in the direction, the provisions of the National Curriculum (a) shall not apply; or (b) shall apply with such modifications as may be so specified'. Such 'directions' will only be given if there is an application by the LEA 'with the agreement of the governing body', or by the Curriculum Council with the agreement of both the LEA and the governing body. The Secretary of State may also make it a condition of a 'direction' that anyone 'by whom or with whose agreement the request for the direction was made' should, when so 'directed' or 'at specified intervals', report to the Secretary of State 'on any matters specified by him'. Unsurprisingly, the Secretary of State may, 'by a direction' vary or 'revoke a direction' made by him under this subsection (of Clause 9).

The way these stringent regulations are formulated hardly indicates that scope will exist under this abhorrent legislation for exercise of initiative by teachers, schools or local authorities. Such a clause could only be formulated by, or gain the approval of, someone totally determined to retain every string in his, or more likely her hands.

# 5 A Constitutional Issue?

In his keynote speech at the Birmingham meeting in October referred to earlier, Sir Peter Newsam raised the constitutional implications of the changes proposed in the Bill. The consultative papers already suggested 'that there are thirty or more examples of new powers for the Secretary of State'. 'What I am concerned about', the former CEO of the ILEA went on, is not the individual operation of these powers, 'but the cumulative effect' in deciding who, in the future, 'will be effectively responsible for what goes on in each individual school' (SCE transcript).

With the actual publication of the Bill at the end of November it immediately became clear that this was an underestimate. The extent of the powers arrogated to the centre over the entire field of the curriculum and assessment has been made abundantly clear in the last chapter. Estimates as to the actual number of new powers to be taken by the Secretary of State vary from a total of 175 (Jack Straw) to 200. Detailed examination of the various clauses and sub-clauses of the Bill indicates that the figure lies somewhere between these two estimates. This is the actual reality of the present situation. Further, as indicated in Chapter 4, assurances by the present Secretary of State, for instance, to the effect that the stringent curriculum proposals will be loosened in practice, have absolutely no status in terms of the legislation itself, and could be abrogated by the present or any future Secretary of State at will. Only the naïve could possibly take such statements at their face value. Present and future Secretaries of State, under the proposed legislation, in fact retain full powers (in the field of curriculum and testing) to do what they like.

Newsam was not the only one to point early to the significance of this development. Another was Tim Brighouse, Chief Education Officer for Oxfordshire.

In early October, he wrote, referring to the present Secretary of State,

> When I hear the honeyed words and see the easy smile, I go back to the detailed words in the consultation document. The Secretary of State ... would have ... a power to appoint governors in grant maintained schools ... to terminate grant ... to set (for all state schools) attainment targets and programmes of study ... to set out arrangements for assessment which schools will follow ... to specify what public qualifications can be offered to pupils ... to approve GCSE syllabuses ... to approve or reject schemes for financial delegation ... to appoint governors to polytechnics and some colleges of further education. (*Observer*, 11 October 1987)

Peter Newsam and Tim Brighouse expressed their fears for the future in different terms, but with similar implications. For Newsam it is not anything the present Secretary of State may do, owing to greatly extended powers, but a future one. At the moment, as he says, 'the constitution contains checks and balances'; but in future 'these powers will be contained within one individual'. We appear to be moving closer to 'direct Ministerial control' of the education service 'and of many of the institutions within it'. That may serve for the present,

> But what if one day this country were to find itself with a Secretary of State possessed of a narrow vision of what education in a democracy should aspire to be, coupled with a degree of self-regard and intolerance of the opinions of others that caused him or her to seek to impose that vision on others?

That is why Newsam argued that ultimately the 'constitutional questions' may prove to be even more important than all the practical aspects, concerning structure, the curriculum, testing, parental choice with which the Bill is overtly directly concerned.

Tim Brighouse, in his newspaper article, strikes a more sombre note. After summarising the new powers allotted to the Secretary of State, he concludes:

> And do you know, I cannot rid myself of images of shirts of black and brown, of echoing footsteps, of clanging doors – all the chilling paraphernalia which, historically, have followed such tidy measures. Suddenly this autumn, after the hurried consultations which didn't quite reach parents in whose name the proposals are made, I taste panic and fear – not for myself but for our grandchildren.

Is that so very far-fetched?

Traditionally – that is historically – over the last 100 years or so, the public system of education in this country has been controlled by a 'partnership', originally of state, local authorities and the voluntary bodies (the churches – particularly the Church of England). Post-war developments, especially the vast expansion of education in the 1950s and 1960s, brought the teachers in as a fourth, but important, 'partner'. It was this partnership, to which lip-service is still paid by Ministers, that used to be celebrated as a leading feature of the British system, as opposed to the highly centralised systems of many other countries. The 'Triple Alliance', as Lester Smith, Manchester's distinguished Director of Education, put it in 1957, had stood the test of time. Since 1870 it had been 'as a bulwark against the winds and waves of controversy', he wrote.

> The tradition of partnership is the outstanding feature of our educational administration. Although we have now endowed the Minister with great power, in practice he and his Ministry of some 3,000 officials function as members of a great fellowship – Ministry, local authorities, teachers, voluntary associations – friends working together with mutual understanding in a great cause.[1]

Writing thirty years ago, he was referring back to the much debated clause of the 1944 Education Act which laid the duty on the Minister of Education to promote education and the progressive development of educational institutions, 'and to secure the effective execution by local authorities, *under his control and direction*, of the national policy' (my emphasis, B.S.). Fears were expressed at the time that the power so accorded was too great, that it 'might open the door to an educational dictatorship', as H.C. Dent then wrote. That fear 'need never be realised, provided Parliament and the public are alive to their responsibilities'. Moreover there was also a safeguard in the provision for two Central Advisory Councils for England and Wales to advise the Minister 'upon such matters connected with educational theory and practice *as they think fit*' (my emphasis, B.S.) as well as on specific questions referred to them. The careful wording was to ensure that matters concerning the curriculum were not subject to the diktat of a politician temporarily in office.[2]

Central Advisory Councils have long since been dispensed with, the Minister of Education has become a Secretary of State. The present government's policy is today marked by sharp antagonism to other members of the 'partnership' – towards local authorities, the teaching profession, even representatives of the churches. The need for the public and its representatives to be 'alive to their responsibilites' in this matter was never greater.

The downgrading of local authorities, politically, financially (rate-capping), through privatisation and in many other ways has been a cumulative process over the past fifteen years or more. Since the demise, in 1972, of the powerful Association of Education Committees, there has been no effective, unified voice presenting, and fighting for, the local authority view on important national issues. There has, also, been a gradual erosion of the influence of the churches, while the teachers have found it increasingly difficult to speak with a single voice and indeed, in terms of organisation, have suffered a process of fragmentation resulting in a gradual decline of influence or political 'clout'. Further, the consistent and hostile criticism of teachers by leading politicians and industrialists, even as they have been forced to resist a policy of eroding pay and degrading conditions of work, has led to a certain demoralisation within the profession, which is another reality to be faced.

Into the vacuum so created the state has moved, specifically the Department of Education and

Science (but also the recently formed Manpower Services Commission) across a wide front and with a certain ruthless energy. The speed of change in this area over the last three or four years has been remarkable. Measures and proposals that would once have been condemned out of hand on all sides, as being not only undesirable in themselves but also impossible to realise politically – total, central (Ministerial) control of the curriculum, for example – are now actually embodied in a Bill before Parliament, which, although hopefully modified, is likely to be carried. Peter Newsam and Tim Brighouse speak for many others who are deeply concerned. It is important that the full implications of what is being prepared are very widely known. This issue cannot be allowed to go by default.

In what sense can this be said to be a constitutional issue? Unlike the United States, where the respective rights and responsibilities of the Federal and State governments are laid down with precision in the constitution (education being among those powers reserved to the states), Britain has no written constitution defining, for instance, the relations between church and state, or those between national and local government nor, for that matter, on any other issue.[3] This is held to be the crowning glory of the British constitution, embodying flexibility, and so allowing for change, while sovereignty lies with Parliament.

The crucial constitutional issues, for instance concerning the relations between Parliament and the monarchy, between church and state, between local and central government, between the state and voluntary associations of all kinds are often embodied in statutes – Acts of Parliament, comprising the laws of Britain, though some important aspects have acquired legal precedent as a result of decisions made by judges, and others are not so crystallised, but handled by conventions. Such relations have developed historically and so become traditional. This is certainly the case in the field of education where the publicly maintained system is by no means correctly defined as a 'state system'. *The Department of Education: a brief guide* (1981 edition), for instance, opens with a chapter entitled 'A National Service Locally Administered', and starts with the words 'The tradition of decentralised education in Britain is strong.'

The 'checks and balances' referred to by Peter Newsam are embodied in the sections of Acts of Parliament, notably now the 1944 Education Act which defines the precise functions of local authorities in the administration of their systems – as also the functions of the state *vis-à-vis* local authorities. By arrogating very many of these powers to the centre, traditional procedures, deriving from earlier Acts of Parliament, are abrogated. In so far as the term 'constitution' refers in the case of Britain to historically developed traditional procedures and precedents, it is evident that Newsam is right to claim that the Education Bill raises constitutional issues, problems or questions (he uses all three terms). It certainly does.

Nor is it only a question of relations between the central authority, local authorities and teachers. Constitutional issues are raised in the important letter to Kenneth Baker from Dr Leonard, Bishop of London, who chairs the Board of Education of the General Synod of the Church of England, cited earlier. Expressing reservations on the matter of opting out (or creating 'grant maintained schools' centrally financed) he asks 'whether there are additional objectives being served by this proposal, to do with relations between national and local government'. It is quite clear, he adds, 'that the effect of large scale adoption of grant maintained status will weaken the position of local government in a fundamental way'. This is a development, he goes on, 'which we would not find acceptable'. The Church of England's Board of Education 'see the maintaining of strong (and responsible) local government *as an essential element in the future of democracy in this country*', adding 'even if we did not, we would still deplore the use of the education system *as a pawn in what was essentially a political intention*' (my emphasis, B.S.).

From this stems what may well be seen as a constitutional issue. 'It is because so many questions ultimately affecting the relationship between church and state (at both local and national level) are involved in the current proposals,' the Bishop of London's letter to the Secretary of State continues, 'that we are disturbed by the speed with which the government is rushing towards legislation.' Preparatory work on the 1944 Education Act took months, not weeks. 'The result was a solid basis of agreement, fully accepted by the church.' The development of a new pattern of educational provision for this country today 'surely requires no less a depth of preparation'. There is here combined an appeal to what may be called agreed constitutional practice, and, at the same time, a warning that the church will not lightly stand aside if historically determined relations are unilaterally abrogated.

After compiling his list of the thirty-three 'new things a Secretary of State is to be responsible for', enumerated in Baker's 'consultative' documents, Sir Peter Newsam asks 'exactly what remains for others to do?' This, he said, is by no means clear. Indeed it is evident, if not glaringly obvious, that apart from carrying out the instructions of central government – while no doubt desperately attempting to maintain their systems as viable – local authorities will have little scope for initiative. The responsibilities of teachers will likewise be severely circumscribed, and limited in the main to the 'delivery' of a curriculum precisely defined from above.

In fact it is local authorities, not central government, that have been responsible for most new initiatives that have been developed historically within the educational system. Once an innovation, first undertaken locally, has shown success and gained widening support it has been the part of central government to add its approbation and incorporate the change in national policy. Many examples could be given, some dating back to the last century but the most recent is the swing to comprehensive secondary education. This was rejected as national policy by both the Labour governments of 1945-51 and the Tory governments from 1951 to 1964. Comprehensive education was initially very much a grass-roots, local authority movement, developed and experimented with from below, in the areas of those few pioneering authorities which insisted on their right to develop this new type of school, then regarded as a radical innovation. First, authorities like Middlesex, the London County Council (as it then was), the West Riding, Coventry and Anglesey developed these schools very effectively, in the late 1940s and 1950s. Then great cities – Manchester, Liverpool, Sheffield, Bradford – insisted on their right to transform their secondary systems, back in 1962-63, well before the next Labour government issued Circular 10/65 requesting authorities to plan to make this change (in July 1965). Other 'structural' initiatives have also resulted from local authority, not central government, action. The whole community school movement, whereby local schools become centres for social, educational and cultural activities stemmed from a Cambridgeshire initiative, led by the Chief Education Officer, Henry Morris, in the 1930s. In the post-war years this idea has been developed afresh in other areas, notably Leicestershire. But this was also a *local* initiative. Even today, local authorities are involved in many new initiatives, not least relating to the curriculum and examinations. Sheffield has a curriculum reform project in both the primary and secondary fields, as has already been noted. In the area of examination reform alternative systems focussing on profiling as a means of assessment – which has many advantages over the old type of written examinations and tests – are being developed by a consortium of four authorities, including Oxfordshire and Leicestershire. This valuable innovation is known as the Oxford Certificate of Educational Achievement. Many other examples could be cited, particularly in the important area of special education for handicapped children in which some authorities have a proud record and have provided an example to follow.

Should a precisely defined national curriculum be imposed, and monitored to ensure that schools adhere to the law, any such initiative on the part of a local education authority would be at risk. The consultation document allots the task of monitoring to school governors but more particularly to Her Majesty's Inspectors whose task it has hitherto been to ensure adequate standards, not enforce a uniform procedure. Even local authority advisers, the document seems to suggest, should cease their current activities of assisting developments in order to police the set curriculum. The question may reasonably be put – what, then, is left for the *teachers* to do?

Their main function, as we have seen, is to 'deliver' the curriculum – or (to use a phrase of Keith Joseph) act as 'agents' for the central authority to ensure that 'delivery'. The consultative document says teachers 'will be free to determine *the detail of what should be taught*' and that 'teaching approaches' are 'also for schools to determine' (my emphasis, B.S.). These can hardly be regarded as liberal concessions. It would hardly be practicable for the most rigidly bureaucratic government to determine 'the detail' of every subject in the curriculum, nor to lay down precisely *how* each teacher should present that or any other 'detail'. These are no more than words introduced to mollify, or mislead – 'see how flexibly minded we are'. Ironically enough, dealing elsewhere with teachers and teaching, the document calls for 'the imaginative application of professional skills at all levels' as the means of 'raising standards'. But what scope will there be for 'imaginative' teaching – presumably what is meant by 'the application of professional skills' – in the new dispensation? All (maintained) schools, throughout the country are to follow the same 'programmes', directed to the same 'attainment targets' and assessed by the same instruments and the same 'nationally prescribed tests'. Is this not a formula for the production of a paralysing uniformity among all schools – *except* of course, the independent schools (to which, as Jack Straw has shown, members of the Cabinet, without exception, send their children) and the city technology colleges.[4] The 'National Curriculum' (not actually 'national'), seems, from this angle, very much like a means of control of 'the masses' (other people's children).

Schools should be the opposite of this – perhaps the precise opposite. They should be lively and stimulating places – not cast in a mould of dead uniformity. Teachers need to feel free to utilise, not only their 'professional skills', but also their creative initiative. To ensure the imaginative involvement of teachers, scope must be given to allow, and to encourage, new developments, new combinations, new procedures. This cannot be achieved when all are bound to rigid, centrally imposed 'programmes', their students' learning monitored by 'nationally prescribed tests' and faceless external examiners (there are *none* of these in Germany, incidentally, a country now often cited as a model by Ministers). It is no wonder that so many of those accepted as leaders of the teaching profession sharply reject this entire approach. Indeed here the comment of George Cooke, recently Chief Education Officer for Lincolnshire, is relevant:

> The most disturbing feature of the present situation is that it is often the most effective and committed teachers who feel most disillusionment. It is almost as if our political leaders (in circumstances not wholly dissimilar from 1939-45) were trying to fight a war calling for great effort and sacrifice without caring a damn for the morale of the fighting troops. (*Education*, 11 July 1986)

These analyses, relating to local authorities and teachers, are not raised as debating points. They relate to the long-term implications of the constitutional changes that are implicit in the Bill, if not there openly proclaimed. Newsam, Brighouse and

Leonard are all concerned with relationships –
between state and local authorities, state and
church, and, it might be added, the state and
teachers who at present are *local authority*
employees. Once the balance of these relations is
radically altered, as is being overtly proposed, the
implications are immense.

It may be that the danger is being exaggerated
here. It may be that, should these proposals be
implemented, there will still be scope for local
authority initiative – or, more likely, that local
authorities will find ways of insisting on space for
manoeuvre within the proposed conditions; and that
teachers will also find ways of giving rein to their
initiative and realising their own goals. The growing
strength of the teacher-researcher movement may
be more powerful than is generally recognised. It
may be that the present government does not yet
realise the likely effect of its actions, and does not
desire it – that, as the *Financial Times* has put it,
Ministers have not thought through their proposals
effectively, or thoroughly, and that, were they to
allow themselves more time to think, ways might be
found of pursuing objectives in a less draconian
manner.

All this *may* be true. Unfortunately, however,
there is little to support this view, either in the
statements of the Secretary of State, nor in those of
the Prime Minister. On the contrary, there is a clear
determination to drive through full centralised
control of almost every aspect of educational
activity, at all levels, throughout the country. And
once these powers have been allotted, through
legislation, to the Secretary of State, what hope is
there that a future holder of the office will
deliberately divest himself or herself of such powers

and generously hand them back? To hold that this may happen is no more than a pipe dream, as also is the theory being bruited abroad (by HMIs and others) that, even after the unmodified passage of the Bill, there is still 'everything to play for'. To hold this view underestimates the steely purpose behind the legislation, and is no more than a comforting piece of self-deception. That, surely, is now very clear indeed.

The drive towards a more rigid, bureaucratised centralism has been a leading feature of the educational world since at least 1976, accelerating rapidly during the past three or four years. In the 1984 edition of the *Brief Guide* issued by the Department of Education and Science, cited earlier, there was already a significant change of emphasis. Both the heading, 'A National Service Locally Administered', and the first sentence, 'The tradition of decentralised education in Britain is strong,' have been deleted. The pamphlet now opens triumphantly: 'The Department of Education and Science is responsible for all aspects of education in England.' Under the present political administration central government no longer desires, let alone accepts, advice, discussion, debate with partners. Nor is it only the schools that are brought to heel but also universities. In the past two years, according to the recently retired chair of the Committee of Vice-Chancellors and Principals, Maurice Shock, 'the ground rules' have dramatically changed. It was his experience that 'a relationship with government which involved argument and debate was now one of increasing control, where debate was no longer tolerated' (*THES*, 13 November 1987). The same is true of all policy areas.

Matters are now moving to a stage when it is for

the public and Parliament to take up the responsibility of defending the educational system and, with this, a constitutional issue of key importance to a democratic order. The honeyed words and easy smile of Kenneth Baker may have misled some into supposing that only self-important educationists could object to his measures. But even in the ranks of his own party, excluded from meaningful discussion as much as anyone else, objections are surfacing. As the Bishop of London and the former Chief Education Officer of the ILEA have effectively warned the country, there is an obligation to question every single aspect of the Thatcher-Baker plan to control the educational system unilaterally from the centre.

Perhaps it might be appropriate to close this chapter with a quotation from an article by the historian, G.M. Trevelyan, entitled 'Stray Thoughts on History':

> Where there is nothing with independent life outside the state machine, civilisation will lose all power of healthy growth. It is from minorities, small groups and individuals that fresh life has always come.[5]

## Notes and References

1 W.O. Lester Smith, *Education, an Introductory Survey*, (Penguin 1957). p. 139.
2 H.C. Dent, *The Education Act 1944* (London 1945), pp. 7-10.
3 In Germany, often held to have a centralised system, responsibility for education is in fact also devolved on the states, in its (written) constitution.
4 The National Association of Primary Education holds that the government's plans for the curriculum 'will encourage only the routine, the unimaginative, the subservient and the time-serving spirits that inspire all of us in the absence of vision and opportunity' (*TES*, 19 October 1987).
5 G.M. Trevelyan, *An Autobiography and Other Essays* (London 1949), pp. 87-8.

# 6 The Education Act and the Future

## 1 The Education Act, 1988

The Education Bill was published on Friday 20 November 1987. Given priority by the government, together with legislation bringing in the poll tax, it passed all its Parliamentary stages in the spring and summer of 1988, finally receiving Royal Assent on 29 July 1988. It is now, therefore, part of the statutory law of the land.

In spite of an overwhelmingly critical response, embodied in what the *Guardian* called 'an unprecedented 16,500 replies' to the original consultation papers, the clauses of the Bill precisely reflected the proposals as originally outlined. The one concession that had been made, though even that was hedged around with qualifications, concerned the time to be devoted to the compulsory element of the 'national curriculum'. There were one or two other minor concessions, as we have seen. But the main thrust of the Bill, concerning structural change in particular, remained unchanged. In particular, no concessions had been made on the two central features of the policy in so far as they concern the schools – open enrolment and opting out.

The Bill's passage through Parliament, and the changes made as a result, are dealt with in a later section of this chapter. Here again these changes hardly affected the main thrust of the Bill, or of the original consultation papers. A new compromise was found on religious instruction. Certain important changes were accepted (largely during the Lords debates) concerning the universities; there were minor (if welcome) changes relating to children with special educational needs. Further, during this period, the working groups concerned with mathematics and science completed their final reports, as did also the Task Group for Assessment and Testing. These flesh out the original proposals and will also be considered below. Finally, during the passage of the Bill, the government accepted an amendment abolishing the ILEA, in place of the original proposals described earlier as 'death by a thousand cuts'. This also will be discussed later.

It may be as well, here, to set out the essential content of the main sections of the Act, under the different headings used in earlier discussion.

### 1 Financial delegation to schools

Sections 33-51 provide that heads and governing bodies will have control over school budgets (see pp. 80-83).

### 2 Open enrolment

Sections 26-32 provide for the lifting of restrictions on the number of pupils schools are allowed to take. The physical capacity of the school in 1979 is to be taken as determining maximum enrolment, although in certain circumstances this may be exceeded (see pp. 59-69).

### 3 Charging for 'extras'

Sections 106-111 cover 'permitted charges', etc., in maintained schools. These sections did not appear in the original Bill, but were introduced as amendments by the government during its passage (see pp. 83-87).

### 4 Opting out ('grant maintained schools')

Sections 52-104 provide that individual schools can leave local authority control, the decision depending on a simple majority of parents voting (as originally outlined in the consultation papers), though with the amendment that, if less than 50 per cent of parents vote, a second ballot is necessary. Application for grant maintained status has to be made by the governing body of the school.

These sections cover the main structural changes affecting schools embodied in the Act. A further section (105) relates to city technology colleges (and city colleges for the technology of the arts). This empowers the Secretary of State to seek financial contracts to fund CTCs, and provides for financial support both for their capital and recurrent costs.

### 5 National curriculum

Sections 1-25 comprise the legislative imposition of a compulsory curriculum consisting of specified subjects, the statutory establishment of the Curriculum Development and Examinations Councils, and wide-ranging empowerment of the Secretary of State to make the various orders required in the future to bring the measure to a conclusion (see pp. 107-122). Sections 6-9 cover collective worship and religious education, while sections 11-13 deal with Standing Advisory Councils on religious education. (These latter sections were added to the original Bill as amendments during its passage.)

### 6 Testing and assessment

Sections 1-25 also provide for equivalent measures relating to testing and assessment of all children at the ages of seven, eleven, fourteen and sixteen.

These two sets of sections cover the government's proposals relating to curriculum and assessment (and religious education) in all maintained schools. As proposed in the original consultation paper, neither independent schools nor city technology colleges are affected by this legislation.

### 7 Abolition of the ILEA

Sections 162-196 provide for the abolition of the ILEA and for the establishment of new local authorities for areas in inner London.

In the field of further and higher education there are four sets of sections.

### 8 Financial delegation in colleges

Sections 139-155 provide for the management of budgets of colleges of further education to become the responsibility of college governing bodies, 50 per cent of whose members are to be drawn from the business world.

### 9 *Independence of polytechnics*

Sections 121-138 provide for the management of all polytechnics and higher education colleges to be removed from the control of local authorities and taken over by governing bodies which must consist of a combination of business people and academics. Sections 132-134 also provide for the establishment of a Polytechnic and Colleges Funding Council, composed of up to nine business people and some others.

### 10 *University grants reform*

Sections 131 and 134 provide for the demise of the University Grants Committee and its substitution by a University Funding Council including a substantial proportion of business people (of the total of fifteen members, at least six must be from commerce and industry).

### 11 *Academic freedom and tenure*

Sections 202-208 provide for the ending of tenure in universities and for the dismissal of staff through redundancy, inefficiency or lack of funds. Section 202 contains the definition of academic freedom accepted by the government during the Bill's passage through the Lords.

The main proposals under (8) and (9) above follow suggestions in the relevant consultation papers very closely, as do those under (10) and (11), though with the amendment outlined above.

## 2 The Bill's Reception

Reception of the Bill by the press can best be
described as somewhat muted. At the launch in a
London hotel Mr Baker was described (by the
*Guardian*) as being 'in a surprisingly subdued mood'
(21 November 1987). The popular, tabloid press,
catering presumably for Baker's 'ordinary people',
clearly and unanimously assessed the
announcement as of *no* interest to its readers. Front
pages were given over to Elton John pulling out of
Watford Football Club (*Sun* and *Mirror*), or to the
Kings Cross tragedy (*Mail* and *Express*). The *Sun*
allotted three inches of small type on an inside page
to Baker's plans; the *Mirror* four inches, also on an
inside page, reporting only Jack Straw's reactions.
The *Express* carried a brief leader supporting Baker
accompanying a little explanatory material on an
inside page. Loyalty to Thatcher no doubt also
determined the *Daily Mail*'s main leader, totally
supporting of the Bill which, it said, 'is fully in tune
with the popular will'.

In the quality press things were different, though
the Bill only made the main front page story in the
*Guardian* (the *Independent* and *Times* focussed on
the Kings Cross disaster, the *Telegraph* on the US
budget deficit). There was, however, editorial
comment in the form of leaders in all four papers,
and considerable detailed coverage of the Bill's
contents. The *Times*, under the heading 'A True
Education Bill' was generally supportive, as was the
*Telegraph*. The *Independent*, whose leader writers
are to be differentiated from its team of educational
reporters, adopted an ambiguous line, concluding
that the clauses of Mr Baker's 'fudged and
uncertain Bill' reflected 'a penny-pinching centra-

lism'. The *Guardian*, under the heading 'The Good, the Bad and the Ugly', while supporting the national curriculum proposals, was very sharply critical of most of the rest, suggesting that the end result of the structural changes would be pandemonium.

An unpleasant feature which now began to surface was a persistent promulgation of the myth that the ills of education are due to the machinations of the so-called 'educational establishment', and that this provides the sole form of opposition to the 'Great Education Reform Bill'. Here the tone had already been set by Kenneth Baker in his speech to the Conservative Party conference early in October. His attack then was focussed on 'the educational establishment' who 'simply refuse to believe that the pursuit of egalitarianism is over'.

> I have to say that we will not tolerate a moment longer the smug complacency of too many educationalists, which has left our national education performance limping along behind that of our industrial competitors. (*Independent*, 8 October 1987)[1]

It is, in fact, the Conservative government that has been responsible for education and its development (or, better, non-development) since 1979 – that is, for almost a decade during which the whole system has consistently been allowed to run down, as described in Chapter 1, until a state of major crisis had been reached by the spring of 1985. More, since 1951, Conservative governments have held the reins of power for twenty-five years out of a total of thirty-six. During this whole period Britain's relative position educationally was allowed to deteriorate on *all* the major criteria as compared to *all* other leading industrial countries.[2] To turn the resultant failures into a cause of criticism and hostility against teachers and local administrators is the height of cynicism, witness to a level of hypocrisy and demagogy both dishonest and incredible. Nevertheless an attempt was made at this point to smear all opposition to the Baker Bill as motivated by the 'vested interests' of the 'educational establishment'.

'Baker Brushes Aside Education Bill Critics', headlined the *Guardian*, reporting the launch (21 November 1987). Responses, numbering 16,000 or more, to the consultation papers could be similarly dismissed; there was, in any case, never any intention to 'consult' as Baker made clear from the start. But now the attack sharpened. The *Telegraph* editorial comment congratulated Baker for 'grappling with that slithery beast, the educational establishment' − a singularly unpleasant and inappropriate metaphor. The government is also congratulated for noting parental wishes rather than those of an establishment 'whose members are expert at delaying tactics'. The *Times* leader is also laced with hostile comments on this 'establishment' thus obediently following the lead of a government determined to rubbish the most informed opposition in these terms, while claiming (with the *Daily Mail*) overwhelming popular support. Radical populism in action, right foot foremost.

## 3 The Broad Alliance

We may examine this charge, that only the 'educational establishment' was opposed to the Bill when it was originally introduced. It is surely significant that all the political parties represented in Parliament, with the single exception of the

Conservative Party, clearly expressed their opposition to the main thrust of the structural changes in the Bill. In particular, open enrolment and opting out were seen as clear threats to the publicly provided school system in an attempt to create the required hierarchical structure (and at the same time deal a strong blow at local education authorities). This was the standpoint of the Labour Party, the Liberal Party and the SDP (as then existing) which together represented nearly 55 per cent of voters in the last election – even if gaining only 40 per cent of seats in the House of Commons. Add the Communist Party and Plaid Cymru – for right across the board there developed a unanimity of political opposition to the main structural proposals. Was all this engineered by the 'educational establishment'?

Secondly, within the Conservative Party itself opposition was expressed, again to the crucial structural changes. In April 1987 the Conservative Education Association was founded, led by Philip Merridale, the Tory leader on the Council of Local Education Authorities and chair of Hampshire Education Committee. The pamphlet then published, *One Last Chance*, boils down to a commitment to the maintained sector of education 'because that is where most parents send their children'. Philip Merridale no doubt 'spoke for them all', writes Barry Hugill, 'when he confessed that his "blood had chilled" on hearing the rapturous applause that Mr. Baker invariably receives when launching blistering attacks on local government' at successive Tory party conferences (*TES*, 3 April 1987).

But Kenneth Baker did not get away with his demagogy at all levels of the Tory Party conference

in the autumn of 1987. Here 'the tradition of
deference' to leaders was 'shattered at a fringe
meeting' at which local party representatives
'repeatedly' expressed concern about the proposed
Education Reform Bill (*TES*, 9 October 1987). Sharp
criticism came from David Muffett, chairman of
Hereford and Worcester Education Committee, and
from Geoffrey Woollard of Cambridgeshire who
'could not see the relevance' to this largely
comprehensive area of 'piecemeal opting out of
schools and the establishment of city technology
colleges'. Further, on the day the Bill was published,
Jack Straw announced that Surrey County Council
(Baker territory) and the Conservative controlled
Barnet council (Thatcherland) were among those
that expressed sharp opposition to the structural
proposals – information gleaned from responses to
consultation papers which it suited the instigators of
the 'Great Reform Bill' to suppress. These changes,
Barnet Council represented, would end 'with a
system loaded against maintained schools in an
indefensibly inequitable manner' and Surrey judged
likewise. Of twenty-two Conservative education
authorities, 'only six were in favour of schools opting
out, but these still voiced criticisms' (*Times*, 21
November 1987).

Total opposition to the proposed structural
changes on the part of Ted Heath was made
abundantly clear as soon as these were announced,
as noted at the outset of this account. Other leading
Tories who expressed doubts and reservations
include Leon Brittan, John Biffen and, to a degree,
Michael Heseltine. In a pamphlet entitled *Chancing
Change* which was published in November 1987,
Andrew Rowe, Tory MP for Mid-Kent, is extremely
critical both of the 'national curriculum' and the

opting out proposals.

That there were dissenting voices within the Tory Party is not surprising. However the main point being made here is that this apparently quite widespread opposition to certain key aspects of the Bill within that party can hardly be written off as manoeuvres on the part of the 'educational establishment'. To the opposition of all other political parties, then, should be added that of a proportion of Conservative supporters, even if, as we shall see, this opposition never manifested itself decisively during the Bill's passage through Parliament.

Thirdly, we may turn to other large, representative organisations. The largest of these, hardly to be categorised as a branch of the 'educational establishment', is the Trades Union Congress uniting over 9,000,000 organised workers and intent on presenting policies in their interests. The critical, and indeed acutely hostile attitude of the TUC to all the main structural proposals of the Bill (not to mention other aspects) has already been referred to. The open entry and opting out proposals were features seen as calculated to undermine the powers of local authorities, to weaken planning, to form a new tier of schools acountable only to the Secretary of State. Late in November 1987 the TUC organised a meeting of all interested organisations as the start of a mass campaign of public meetings against the Bill. The object was to ensure that such a meeting was held 'in every school, college, polytechnic, students' union, town hall or community centre' with a mass rally in London. The Education Alliance, an umbrella group for trade unions, student and education groups, was re-established at regional and local level, leaflets provided and

widespread action undertaken (*Educational Brief-
ing*, TUC, No.1, November 1987).

The Church of England, as we have seen, took a
very critical stance, as did other churches. There is
no need to reiterate here the unrelenting analysis of
all key aspects of the Bill, by no means solely on the
issue of religious instruction, in the letter from the
Bishop of London to Kenneth Baker. But it should
be underlined that the views expressed were those of
the Board of Education of the Synod of the Church of
England which is broadly representative of the
church as a whole. Manifestly to categorise the
Anglican church as an element of the 'educational
establishment' is to deprive the term of all meaning.

Fourth, what of the parents and their organisations? Whatever the government may seek to
claim, and the tabloid press declare, no parental
groups or their organisations came to the fore when
the Bill was launched to welcome the offer to
parents to take over the running of local schools,
lock, stock and barrel. On the other hand all
organisations which have to do with parents
expressed profound anxiety about the main thrust of
government proposals and with this proposition.
This is the case of the National Confederation of
Parent Teacher Organisations, which can certainly
claim to be a mass, representative (and democratically run) organisation – it has been unrelentingly
hostile to the proposals from their inception. The
Campaign for the Advancement of State Education
is largely a middle-class parental pressure group
concerned to strengthen the publicly provided
system, but cannot be placed within the 'educational
establishment'; nor, for that matter, can the
Advisory Centre for Education, an independent
organisation whose main function is to counsel

parents and which can itself be critical of schools, but presently concentrates criticism on government strategy and tactics.

Finally, there are the local authorities and teachers. Here, perhaps, is the real 'educational establishment' pursued by Baker and the *Daily Telegraph*. Certainly there is an interest in these quarters in the prevailing system – perhaps even a 'vested' interest. It may be argued that restrictive attitudes have existed and do exist here, and, too, a tendency to conservatism. On the other hand the very great majority of local authorities have carried out their statutory responsibilities very effectively, throughout their history – only a small minority have been open to complaints, and this has been a very recent phenomenon. Teachers' organisations have similarly played a central role in the development of national education, in the defence and improvement of the whole structure of maintained schooling – not least in the teeth of operations by penny-pinching Ministers and central administrators. To identify with the schools you serve, to fight for their interests and a better service for the children within them and the parents of those children is not a matter of 'vested' interest. That is to be discerned, with great clarity, in Mrs Thatcher's claim that the national schools and those they serve are at her disposition when she seeks to contain, if not destroy, Labour controlled local authorities. By contrast what teachers and local authorities seek is that the health and viability of the public system of education be put first.

In sum, a very widely representative, broad alliance of organisations and individuals, crossing a wide spectrum of interests and outlook, united in hostility to the main thrust of the Baker Bill. It was in the process of defining an approach, in response to the consultation papers, on the part of each individual organisation separately, that views were consolidated which turned out to be in agreement on the key issues. What emerged was an astonishingly high level and degree of unity in opposition, one positive outcome of the government's bogus arrangements for 'consultation'.

This opposition expressed itself in various ways during the passage of the Bill through Parliament. Mass rallies, meetings and conferences were organised on both a local and national scale. In March the National Union of Teachers ran its Albert Hall rally, the Trades Union Congress its Parliamentary lobby and mass rally at Westminster Hall. The National Union of Students was also active, organising demonstrations and meetings both locally and nationally. In March, also, a 'demonstrative conference' attended by over 500, was held at Friends House in London, organised by the independent educational journal *Forum*. This was typical in that this protest against the Bill was carried through in co-operation with 26 national organisations, including all the main teachers' and parents' organisations, labour movement organisations (NALGO and NUPE), local authorities as well as a variety of social organisations. A declaration of intent embodying desired changes in the Bill, and proposing specific forms of action if the Bill was passed unamended, was carried by acclamation.[3]

## 4  The Bill in Parliament

The Parliamentary battle opened on 1 December with the debate on the Second Reading in the House of Commons. This was overshadowed, at least in its reporting, by what the *Independent* described as a 'blistering attack' by Ted Heath, from the Conservative benches, on the Bill as a whole. Its espousal of parental choice, was, according to Heath, 'largely a confidence trick', while opting out was part of a policy which would inevitably lead to selection and fee-paying (2 December 1987). Heath further attacked the proposal to 'dictate' to universities what they could do and how they were going to do it, while the Secretary of State for Education and Science was accused of taking more power than any other member of the Cabinet – 'more power than the Chancellor, more power than the Secretary of State for Defence. More power than the Secretary of State for Social Services – and direct power too.' That is why academics have not spoken out – 'because they are afraid they are going to lose their jobs'. The proposals, Heath added, are 'divisive', and 'would be fatal to a large number of children'. The Bill, which could not be compared to earlier ones, was contrary to the 'One Nation' Tory tradition. Parent power 'is just a political slogan of no real meaning as far as the educational system today is concerned'. 93 per cent of parents already got the school of their choice; headteachers did not want financial control of their schools, nor did governors. The Bill would 'undermine and destroy the educational system'.

This full-blooded assault could have been foreseen from Heath's first intervention following the Queen's speech in July 1987. As a product of the maintained system himself, and with a record of support for comprehensive schools, Heath's attack carried conviction, perhaps more especially outside the House. Within it he was, of course, rubbished by Norman Tebbit, and it was this that made the headlines the next day. Again, generally, the tabloid press evaluated this 'Great Education Reform Bill' as of no interest to its readers. The *Sun* made no mention whatever of the debate. The *Mirror* rated it more highly, giving it one column inch under the heading 'Ted Canes 'em'. The *Daily Mail* used the occasion to slam Heath (his 'vitriolic and resentful broadside rebounded on him'), though their Parliamentary correspondent, under the heading, 'Baker's Big Day' indicated that Mr Baker himself was constantly in view 'polite, smiling, suave, gently amusing, persuasive, selected by ability, like the floor manager of a most superior gents outfitter' (2 December 1987). No attempt was made, this time round, to present the Bill as the 'will of the people'. An unrepentant Heath continued his attack the next day in a BBC radio interview. The real purpose of the legislation, he now said, was Mrs Thatcher's desire to create a network of fee-paying schools.

> I'm strongly opposed to it because it means the poor, the less well off, are going to be the ones who suffer. That's not what Conservative education policy has been about in the past or should be about today. (*Guardian*, 3 December 1987)

The government carried the second reading by 348 votes to 241, a majority of 107. Ted Heath was the only Conservative to abstain 'as Tory colleagues bayed and barracked on the backbenches' (*TES*, 4 December 1987).

The Bill now went to the Commons Committee, where it ceased to make headline news. In spite of weeks of intensive meetings, often into the small hours in the morning, not a single concession of any importance was made by the government – or, to put the matter obversely, not a single gain, in the form of an amendment, was achieved by the opposition, cf course greatly outnumbered in terms of voting power. The only chance of any serious change in the Bill's contents depended entirely on dissident votes by some of the Committee's Tory members. In no other way was a majority against the government a possibility. Press reports indicated that two or three possible revolts, in this sense, were effectively contained by the government. The opposition's declared aim was to win the argument, if it could not win majorities for amendments. To some extent this objective was achieved.

However that may be, the Bill was returned to the full House virtually unchanged. It was in the final debate on the report stage that the government permitted a raid by two ex-Ministers which resulted in writing into the Bill measures involving the actual *abolition* of the Inner London Education Authority, in place of its death by a thousand cuts as outlined in Chapter 3. Michael Heseltine and Norman Tebbit were the instigators – for political reasons which were argued at length in the press. In response, outraged London parents immediately organised an intensive ballot of those involved – Londoners with children in ILEA schools – supervised by the respected Electoral Reform Society. This returned a massive vote against the decision. 94 per cent of those voting (137,000 parents) overtly rejected the proposition, only 8,000 accepted it, or 5.5 per cent – a majority of 19 to 1. The vote drew a proportion of 55 per cent of those eligible to vote – much higher than normally achieved in local elections.

This, then, was the only major change when the Bill passed the Commons. It now moved to the Lords.

It was here, of course, that opponents of the Bill

hoped to achieve some successes with a series of amendments which could draw the teeth of the Bill itself, particularly as regards its structural aspects. Lord Whitelaw had suggested that two aspects of the Bill might well face defeat in the Lords – the (original) proposals relating to the ILEA, and the opting out clauses. The Bill had its First Reading in the Lords, involving a full-scale debate, in April. Conflicts on the ILEA, opting out, religious education and certain aspects of the clauses relating to universities were here presaged. The Bill moved to the Committee of the House early in May. Unlike procedure in the Commons, the Committee of the Lords consists of the full House. There followed several weeks of intensive debate on every aspect of the Bill.

When presented to the Lords, the Bill had grown from its original 137 clauses to 198. This was not, of course, the result of opposition amendments being incorporated, since none were passed. The massively increased size of the Bill was due to a great number of detailed government amendments considered necessary for the precise definition of functions and procedures, and in every case submitted by the government itself, and accepted by the full House of Commons. Many of these new amendments had been dealt with at breakneck speed in the Commons during the final two or three days' debate on the report stage.

There is not space here to deal in any detail with the debates in the Lords, where it did appear that a chance existed of obtaining substantial amendments to the most damaging clauses. This was because, apart from the Labour peers (about 120, Liberal and SDP peers also opposed the Bill, the bishops were known to be antagonistic to certain aspects, e.g. opting out, while about 250 peers sit on the cross-benches and owe allegiance to no political party. Further, some Conservative peers had publicly expressed opposition to certain clauses of the Bill. It seemed, therefore, that the situation there was more open than in the Commons, although of course the Commons has powers to reject Lords amendments.

Although a doughty battle was put up, particularly by the Labour and SDP opposition, but by others also on certain issues, as far as the main thrust of the Bill embodied in the schools clauses are concerned, only one major victory was achieved. This concerned procedures relating to opting out, and laid it down that, in the ballot of parents relating to this issue, this would only have validity if more than 50 per cent of all parents registered voted in the ballot. To move ahead for a moment, this was modified later in the Commons by an amendment stating that, if less than 50 per cent of parents voted in a first ballot, then a second had to be held within fourteen days.

So far as the main measures affecting schools are concerned, then, the Bill was successfully piloted through the Lords by the government, all these gaining assent. An amendment on the ILEA, asking that there should be a pause for reconsideration before abolition, which gained widespread cross-bench and independent support, was in fact voted down. This was achieved by the mobilisation of a large number of usually non-attending 'backwoods' peers on the night of the vote (equivalent, or nearly so, to the massive mobilisation of such peers a week later to vote down Lord Chelwood's motion, again asking for a pause and rethink on the poll tax). In this connection Lord Hailsham's characterisation of a previous government as an 'elective dictatorship' was widely cited. The government legitimately (but perhaps not altogether democratically) relied on its 100-plus majority in the Commons to force through the Bill there. In the Lords it relied on the in-built majority of hereditary peers, only a proportion of whom normally attend, to force through aspects, or measures, seen generally as highly controversial.[4]

The government did, however, accept certain amendments in the Lords pressed very strongly by the universities, which are well represented there. These concerned writing a definition of academic freedom on to 'the face of the Bill' (as the phrase goes) – this relates to the Bill's abolition of tenure at universities. Other minor concessions concerned clauses related to funding. Further, as concerns the schools, much time in the Lords was spent on the issue of religious education (almost totally ignored in the original Bill), particularly the inclusion of collective worship 'wholly or mainly of a broadly Christian character'. Here a compromise solution was finally found largely through the diplomatic skills of the Bishop of London. But this issue is tangential to the main concerns of this book, so will not be explored further.

A few minor gains were made (in the sense of government amendments) which one hopes will improve the position of children with special educational needs. Those specifically concerned and knowledgeable about the problems here made an energetic attempt to achieve changes they thought desirable. They were, it seems, only partially successful.[5]

As must be clear from this analysis, necessarily brief, in spite of the opposition engendered in the country described earlier, and of the efforts of the opposition parties and others in Parliament, the Bill in fact passed successfully though all its stages by mid-summer. The final debates in the House of Commons took place late in July. The Bill gained Royal Assent on 29 July. Although an enormous measure (a 'Gothic monstrosity' in Peter Wilby's words), it had been pushed through Parliament at great speed, as always had been the intention. It now took its place on the statute book.

## 5   Implementing the Act

The 'steely purpose' shown in the way the government drove the Bill virtually unchanged through Parliament has been shown also in the actions taken immediately after (and in some cases even before) the Bill received Royal Assent. These relate specifically to measures concerned directly with the main thrust of the Act: local financial management, grant-maintained schools and opting out, as also to City Technology Colleges. In the area of the curriculum (and testing) a number of actions were also put in hand with great rapidity. It is important that all should be clear about the nature and probable impact of these actions, so that steps can be taken by those concerned to defend and extend fully comprehensive systems under local control. The current actions put these at risk – and are designed to do just this. The struggles around these actions will determine the future.

These issues will be discussed in turn, starting with structural questions.

*(i)  Local financial management and opting
out*

Problems relating to local financial management
(LFM) (devolution of budgetary control to individual
schools and governing bodies) are extremely complex, nor are many crucial issues, e.g. relating to the
formula governing payments yet determined. Local
authority schemes for implementing local financial
management have to be submitted to the DES by 30
September 1989. The shortness of the time allowed
is putting extreme pressure on local authorities.
Further, as Jackson Hall has pointed out in a
penetrating and detailed article, it seems probable
that the actual implementation of LFM will
introduce new forms of discrimination between
locally provided schools.[6]

Although it has been argued in this book that
LFM is not necessarily a threat to local systems in
itself, its actual implementation needs most careful
monitoring over the years to come – particularly in
terms of the actual formulas governing payments to
schools finally introduced by this government.

Of greater immediate importance, however, are
government actions relating to opting out. All critics
of the Bill and Act see these sections as by far the
most damaging in terms of the health and viability
of local authority systems, and especially where, as
in the great majority of cases, these are systems of
comprehensive primary and secondary schools. The
arguments won't be reiterated here, but the deep
concern relating to these clauses of the Bill were
very clearly shown from the moment the consultation paper making these proposals were first
issued (see pp. 47-48).

Here the government has lost no time at all, and is

now engaged in an overt, and even brazen, campaign against local authorities in an effort to prise local schools from their control. Already before the Bill passed through Parliament, a unit was set up with the full support of the DES (though stated to be independent from it) to propagate and drive through this policy. This is called the 'Grant Maintained Trust', and has the function of giving advice and support to local authority schools considering opting out.

Already by the end of August (that is, at the start of the school year) this body circulated all relevant primary and secondary schools (and chairs of governing bodies) with a glossy pamphlet twelve pages long, embellished with photos and other attractive material, e.g. red ticks, the whole being entitled 'The New Choice in Education – opt out' (red tick against these words). The argument presented overtly denigrates local authorities, impugning the value and effectiveness of their work. In a section entitled 'The Opportunity Ahead', the pamphlet states 'grant maintained status gives to governors, heads and parents the opportunity to improve the quality of education on offer at their schools unhindered by local authority pressure'. The pamphlet specifically invites schools threatened by what the pamphlet calls 'adverse reorganisation' to consider opting out – a clear invitation to use opting out as a means of sabotaging local plans for the rationalisation of facilities in the interests of local children as a whole. This pamphlet, circulated directly to schools (apparently addressed to heads), and not through the local authorities despatch systems appears as an extraordinary action for a responsible body having government support to take – a direct attempt to destabilise local authorities, and through this, local systems. This is a sharply aggressive measure and should be recognised as such. It requires an equally aggressive response.

But this is not all. The application to opt out, as we have seen, must be made by the governing body, after carrying through the parents' ballot(s) as set out earlier. To get rapid decisions (and this is clearly a political imperative – political futures depend on it) governing bodies have to meet. But here there is a snag, unfortunate for this government. The *1986* Education Act provided for the reconstitution of governing bodies, reducing local authority representation and increasing that of parents. This reconstitution was timed for the autumn of 1988 – just the moment when the glossy pamphlet just mentioned descended on the schools. But at this moment, few of the reconstituted governing bodies in fact yet existed.

The result had been an undignified pressure by the government on local authorities in an attempt to ensure that governing bodies are reconstituted with the utmost speed, procedures being suggested which appear to cut across legally acceptable norms. It appears as I write that local authorities, dismayed by the upsetting of orderly procedures, are considering legal action.[7] Whatever the outcome, the main thrust of all this is very clear. It is to pressurise newly constituted governing bodies into immediate decisions relating to opting out, and is therefore an attempt to rush things through with the utmost celerity.

But a decision relating to opting out is one of the utmost importance for any school, and requires the most careful consideration, at the very least. By attempting to ride in this cavalier (and thoroughly unstatesmanlike) manner over accepted procedures, the government is showing its hand only too clearly, and appearing as dangerously irresponsible in its methods and procedures.

What can be done about this? The issue of opting out will remain on the agenda now for the whole of the foreseeable future. It will act as a continuing threat to the viability (and unity) of local authority systems. What needs to be made absolutely clear is that the statutory position is that schools (or governing bodies) may decide whether or not to apply to opt out. Those who wish to preserve and develop their local comprehensive systems have a perfect constitutional right to counter propaganda or activities of the kind referred to above in whatever ways they find most effective. The Association of Metropolitan Authorities is carrying through just such a campaign, and intends to continue to do so in the futur. Others also are concerned, e.g. parents' associations and teachers. Such action needs to get off the ground as early as possible, and to be consistently maintained over the future. The case for the defence of local systems of primary and secondary education needs to be put at least as strongly and effectively as the alternative, if possible – more so.

In defending local systems, a deep defensive structure can be built around the schools, involving parents and their organisations, governing bodies and their organisations, teachers, the churches and local community organisations of all kinds. It is likely that the government's intentions can only be thwarted if a sufficient head of steam can be generated locally in opposition to actions that may well appear both cynical and irresponsible.

In order to win the opting out battle, the government has taken another seemingly highly irresponsible action. This is to declare what has been described as a 'planning blight' until 31 December 1988 (six months) on local authority reorganisation plans. The object of this action appears to be precisely to allow schools threatened (if that is the right word) with reorganisation, for instance within tertiary systems, to apply for grant maintained status in order to remain as they are. This action is directly related to the undignified rush and pressure for the reconstitution of governing bodies, since a time limit for this blight clearly had to be set (though presumably it could be extended). This action, incidentally, underlines the correctness of Anne Sofer's early prediction (see pp. 70-71) that the opting out clauses of the Bill would prove to be, in practice, a profoundly *conservative* measure (in the sense of ensuring that things remain as they are). 'The charge towards opting out puts a total planning blight on the whole of school reorganisation in the country', commented Gordon Cunningham, Education Officer of the Association of County Councils (*Education*, 12 August 1988). So much for the governments vaunted 'radicalism'.

These post-Act actions by the government are sharp and exceptionally aggressive – indeed could almost be described in terms of the deliberate sabotage of local systems. They are extraordinary acts to be taken in the name of the state since the state, or government, has overall responsibility for the health and effective functioning of the nation's system as a whole. Rationalisation of local systems is absolutely necessary, as the government's own Audit Commission frequently points out. Nevertheless all this is pushed aside in what appears as an overall scramble for political advantage.

## (ii) City technology colleges

Here the case is different. The initiative to set up such colleges does not rest with local authorities in any sense. It rests with the Secretary of State, since a section of the Act specifically legitimates these colleges and permits finance from the Exchequer to be used both for capital costs and recurrent expenditure – though initially it was announced that all capital costs would be borne by industry. In spite of this change, Kenneth Baker has claimed that 'The government has had more support for city technology colleges than for any other venture this century.' (*Independent*, 5 September 1988). This hyperbole seems unbelievable. Further it is common knowledge that it does not square with the facts.

Here again, another semi-official body or trust, again publicly funded, has been established to press forward in all sorts of ways with this initiative. It is necessary, therefore, to assess realistically the degree of determination being shown here also in the erection of this important addition to Margaret Thatcher's third tier in the hierarchic system (see p. 16). But few authorties, whatever their political complexion, are likely to welcome a CTC in their area, and very few have (though Solihull is once more an exception). Whatever may be the case for the establishment of such institutions (and a credible case is still wanting), few authorities could easily assimilate such a cuckoo's egg in its nest without serious disruption of their existing systems of secondary education. This is a major objection to this initiative. Many hold that the money to be made available for financing these colleges (actually schools), most of which will now come from the

Exchequer, would be far better spent in funding rather more effectively the existing schools for the mass of ordinary children. It is worth noting that the House of Commons public accounts committee is to investigate the financial implications of the whole, now increasingly expensive, project.[8] The fact that the first of these schools, that at Solihull, was over-subscribed and so had to devise means of selection, is now triumphantly asserted by Kenneth Baker as a desirable outcome. If these schools really do imply a return to selection (as seems probable and desired by the government) then it seems odd that Britain is the only advanced industrial country (so far as I know) seriously planning such a return, if by these devious routes. This initiative clearly needs to be carefully watched and monitored by those with the interests of local systems, which must cater for all, at heart. Although in a sense this overblown initiative is at present conceived as functioning only on a small scale (targets being twenty schools by the early 1990s, catering for 20,000 pupils), it clearly has scope for further expansion.

### (iii)  Curriculum and testing

There is not space here, unfortunately, to go into the plans for the statutory imposition of the 'National Curriculum', with its attendant procedures for testing and assessment of all children at the ages of seven, eleven, fourteen and sixteen. The National Curriculum Council and the School Examinations and Assessment Council, were both appointed shortly after the passage of the Act, *all* members of *both* bodies being nominees of the Secretary of State. The Task Group on Assessment and Testing (TGAT) presented an interim report early in 1988, and its final report(s) in the summer (see p. 112). The proposals made (for 'formative' assessment) were more liberal than had been expected, though experts still had many reservations as to the overall impact of the scheme.[9] The group supported the proposal that test results of schools should be published, including those for seven-year-olds. The scheme proposed will categorise all pupils by the age of sixteen on a ten-point scale. There are, however, still many aspects of the scheme to be worked out in the future (relating to subject testing), nor is it known (at the time of writing) whether the Secretary of State fully accepts the TGAT proposals, nor what modifications he may make in the final Orders. It will be remembered that a sharp division of opinion emerged between Margaret Thatcher and Kenneth Baker on this issue, the former (in a leaked letter) stressing the need for nationally prescribed pencil and paper tests of the traditional kind, in contradistinction to the TGAT proposals. Outcomes relating to assessment and testing, therefore, remain to be determined.

As regards the actual content of the curriculum, the working parties on mathematics and science (see p. 111) submitted their interim reports at the end of December (1987), and their final reports in the summer of 1988. Consultation procedures, as laid down in the Act, are being carried through during the autumn, and outcomes may be known by the time this revised edition appears. The working party on English, appointed in the summer, is also expected to report during the late autumn of 1988 and similar consultation procedures will then be gone through. The intention is to set up further working groups covering the other subjects later. Here again, it is not known at the time of writing whether the Secretary of State will accept these reports, nor what modifications he may make in the final Orders over which he has total control (he has powers to modify or reject any advice offered, see p. 134). As is well known, there are many problems as to whether an adequate supply of qualified teachers exists to implement the national curriculum as laid down by the Act, particularly in the areas of science, modern languages and mathematics. Nevertheless it is intended to bring in the new curriculum and testing procedures by a series of measures over the next few years, starting in September 1990, when the core and other foundation subjects are to be studied 'for a reasonable time' in all maintained schools.

The nature and impact of the whole curriculum and testing measures embodied in the Act deserve a book to themselves. No doubt several such will be written over the coming years.

## 6  Perspectives for the Future

What of the future? It now seems very clear that, as regards the public provision of education, two principles stand opposed. The Education Act is fuelled by a certain ideology – that of the market-place. Its progenitors put their faith in competition, as Kenneth Baker has stressed time and again. Local financial management, open enrolment, grant maintained schools, even city technology colleges are all rationalised on the ground that the resulting competitive battles for 'customers' between schools (seen almost as independent corporations) must inevitably result in the general improvement of educational practice and in the enhancement of standards. Good schools will drive out bad. Popular schools will expand, increase their prestige, flourish (some may even become independent), while 'unpopular' schools (mostly in inner cities, in all probability) will go into a spiral of decline, of low morale, and eventually, ceasing to be viable, will close. Such, at least, seems the desired scenario. So, according to this doctrine (though this must surely be an act of faith), overall, everything will get better. These conditions generally imply, as an essential aspect of this strategy, prising the schools loose from the local authorities. The chosen instruments to achieve this are the parents. This market-place philosophy, incidentally, has been brilliantly analysed by Ted Wragg, in the pamphlet he wrote for the NUT (*Education in the Market Place: the ideology behind the 1988 Education Bill*).

The other principle is the direct opposite of this. Its watchword is co-operation, rather than competition (though this does not exclude emulation, a more appropriate term, perhaps, when considering education). The principle, as I see it, is acceptance of responsibility for the equal provision of a public good – education, health or whatever. As Tawney once wrote, 'What a wise parent desires for his child, the state will desire for all its citizens.' Jackson Hall, ex-Chair of the Society of Education Officers, in the article cited earlier on local financial management, in which he showed its potential for enhancing differentiation between schools, put the matter quite clearly. The local education authority has a responsibility for the provision of education equally for all – and the emphasis is on the words *for all*.[10]

It may be that there could be principled exceptions to this – exceptions which can be defended and argued on rational grounds and which come to achieve general acceptance. An example might be a policy of positive discrimination, as advocated by the Plowden Committee, and implemented to some extent in the education priority areas, by which a higher than average proportion of available resources are allocated to particular groups of children – in this case defined as deprived, or disadvantaged. But apart from such rationally conceived exceptions, the principle must be the *equal* provision of resources (which must be scarce) to *all*. In fact, this concept was written into the 1944 Education Act, with its perspective of secondary education for all. On what other principle could the public provision of education find its justification – particularly in time of war, when equal sacrifices were demanded, and as freely given?

The market place philosophy cannot of course lead to equality of provision and does not seek to. The enhanced competitive process envisaged must inevitably result in the arrangement of schools in a hierarchy. That is its intention. To achieve this, schools must be released from the supposedly malign grip of local authorities. It is now parents (as governors) who are to run the schools.[11] Parents are thus counterposed, as a force, to local authorities. Schools are set to become semi-independent corporate bodies (or little business). These must compete with each other in order to remain viable – and in a period of rapidly falling rolls in the immediately future in most areas. So the scene is set for the battles of the future.

The main objective of these struggles, for those who wish to maintain and strengthen existing comprehensive systems of both primary and secondary education, must then be to strengthen the role of local authorities, as the essential base for systems of education under local, democratic control. Enlightened parents, who see the importance of local democracy, must play their part in these future struggles by taking on the job of governors in schools, onerous though it may prove to be. It can also be rewarding. In any case there is certainly an important job to be done in this area by those deeply concerned about the future of our schools.

A positive outcome from these developments could well emerge from the welding of new relations between teachers, parents and the community as a whole in defence of local schools and school systems. A parent body that consciously decides *not* to opt out, probably against national and local propaganda to do so, is deliberately taking a stand *in support of* its local authority. Relations between teachers, parents and governing bodies are likely to be enhanced by such deliberate action. The whole movement for constructive involvement of parents in the activities of schools, developed greatly in recent years, can be furthered and the basis laid for schools to develop as community schools, serving both children and adults in the neighbourhood, as, of course, is already the case in some areas of the country. From the present crisis, positive outcomes may be achieved. But only provided those accepting the analysis of this book do not relax, even for a single instant; but continue to monitor everything with eagle eyes, and react accordingly, and according to principle. In that direction there lies a hope for the future.

## Notes and References

1 However, typically, when challenged after the launch of the Bill in a BBC television programme (22 November 1987), Baker said he believed in equality of opportunity, *and* claimed that his Bill would enhance it.

2 For instance, in 1981-83, the percentage of boys and girls in full-time education and training at eighteen in the United Kingdom was at the bottom of the list in EEC countries at 17.8 and 16.8 respectively. Most other countries had well over 40 per cent in both categories, with Denmark at the top with over 60 per cent. Japan retains about 90 per cent in full time education at school until 18, as does also the USA. Eurostats, *Education and Training* 1985, Table 5. These figures exclude YTS which is not recognised in the EEC as full-time training. Figures relating to the percentage of a generation (at higher education age range) entering university (in 1980) again show the UK at the bottom of the list with 9.3 per cent compared to 27.8) per cent in the USA and 25.5 per cent in Japan (and 21.3 per cent in France). See A.D. Green, 'Lessons in Standards', *Marxism Today*, January 1988.

3 A full report of this conference, by Edward Blishen, is in *Forum*, Vol.30, No.3, together with the declaration of intent.

4 On this issue, Baroness Warnock writes that many of the opposition and cross-bench peers have been 'outraged ... by the power of the government, in the end, to win a vote by whipping in those hereditary peers who seldom or never appear except when so instructed, and who know nothing whatever about the subject of the debate'. There were several such occasions, she adds, 'in the troubled passage of the recent education bill through the House. It is hard at such times not to despair of the system.' *New Statesman*, 16 September 1988.

5 See Klaus Wedell, 'Special Educational Needs and the Education Reform Act', *Forum*, Vol.31, No.1, Autumn 1988, for a critical evaluation of the impact of the Act on children with special educational needs. Klaus Wedell is Professor of Educational Psychology at the University of London Institute of Education.

6 Hall concludes by saying that LFM 'is what it is in its nature to be – a motor of differentiation and inequality'. 'Directed to the Wrong Church', *Times Educational Supplement*, 5 August 1988. LFM is to be implemented by April 1993.

7 *Education*, 9 September 1988; see also ibid., 2 September 1988.

8 Peter Wilby, 'In the Shadow of Baker's Pets', *Independent*, 15 September 1988. This article makes a cool assessment of the whole project.

9 Harry Torrance (ed.), *National Assessment and Testing: a Research Response*, British Educational Research Association, April 1988.

10 Jackson Hall, op. cit., (note 6). His argument is that local authorities have always stood for equity. 'To the LEA, equity is fairness to the community, all of it.'

11 Though Kenneth Baker has recently indicated that it will be head-teachers who will run the schools. Circular 7/88, published early in September, provides for the devolution of this responsibility by governing bodies precisely on to the heads.

*also available*

## Does Education Matter?

### Brian Simon

In this highly acclaimed set of essays Britain's leading historian of education examines some of the most pressing problems facing everyone concerned with education – teachers, students and parents. An ardent advocate of local control of education and the comprehensive system, Brian Simon explores the roles played by teachers and local authorities in moulding British education, and also looks at the first moves by the Thatcher government towards centralised control of education and the effects of cuts in schooling.

Brian Simon argues that education, in combination with other social forces, can be a powerful agent for change. An effective educational system involves a psychological approach which recognises human potential and the establishing of workable pedagogical means by which teaching is developed so that all can have access to science and culture. What this involves is discussed in this book, which takes as its starting point that education does matter – and matters very much!

'A beautifully written and well pointed series of analyses' – Maurice Kogan, *Journal of Curriculum Studies*

*£6.95 paperback*

# Studies in the History of Education

## Brian Simon

### The Two Nations and the Educational Structure, 1780-1870

This first volume of the standard work on the history of education in England traces the emergence of modern education from the efforts of the scientific societies of the 1780s to the securing of universal education with the Act of 1870.

### Education and the Labour Movement, 1870-1920

The period of Britain's imperial heyday was characterised by the efforts of organised labour to do away with class privilege in education, but in fact saw the consolidation of a divided system of educational provision with the mass of children receiving no more than an 'elementary' education and the privileged few being prepared for university.

### The Politics of Educational Reform, 1920-1940

The inter-war period was a contradictory one in the history of education; while financial cuts were imposed during the depression, and 'intelligence tests' developed which exacerbated the already hierarchic educational system, the ground was also prepared for the reforming Education Act of 1944.

*£6.95 paperback each*